A Facing History and Ourselves Study Guide

TEACHING REPORTER

A STUDY GUIDE CREATED TO ACCOMPANY
THE FILM **REPORTER**

FACING HISTORY AND OURSELVES

Facing History and Ourselves is an international educational and professional development organization whose mission is to engage students of diverse backgrounds in an examination of racism, prejudice, and antisemitism in order to promote the development of a more humane and informed citizenry. By studying the historical development of the Holocaust and other examples of genocide, students make the essential connection between history and the moral choices they confront in their own lives. For more information about Facing History and Ourselves, please visit our website at *www.facinghistory.org*.

Copyright © 2010 by Facing History and Ourselves National Foundation, Inc. All rights reserved.

Facing History and Ourselves® is a trademark registered in the US Patent & Trademark Office.

Cover photos courtesy of Will Okun (*www.wjzo.com*).

To order classroom copies, please fax a purchase order to 617-232-0281 or call 1-800-856-9039 to place a phone order.

To receive additional copies of this resource, please visit *reporter.facinghistory.org*.
ISBN-13: 978-0-9819543-5-6

Facing History and Ourselves Headquarters
16 Hurd Road
Brookline, MA 02445-6919

ABOUT FACING HISTORY AND OURSELVES

Facing History and Ourselves is a nonprofit educational organization whose mission is to engage students of diverse backgrounds in an examination of racism, prejudice, and antisemitism in order to promote a more humane and informed citizenry. As the name Facing History and Ourselves implies, the organization helps teachers and their students make the essential connections between history and the moral choices they confront in their own lives, and offers a framework and a vocabulary for analyzing the meaning and responsibility of citizenship and the tools to recognize bigotry and indifference in their own worlds. Through a rigorous examination of the failure of democracy in Germany during the 1920s and '30s and the steps leading to the Holocaust, along with other examples of hatred, collective violence, and genocide in the past century, Facing History and Ourselves provides educators with tools for teaching history and ethics, and for helping their students learn to combat prejudice with compassion, indifference with participation, myth and misinformation with knowledge.

Believing that no classroom exists in isolation, Facing History and Ourselves offers programs and materials to a broad audience of students, parents, teachers, civic leaders, and all of those who play a role in the education of young people. Through significant higher education partnerships, Facing History and Ourselves also reaches and impacts teachers before they enter their classrooms.

By studying the choices that led to critical episodes in history, students learn how issues of identity and membership, ethics and judgment have meaning today and in the future. Facing History and Ourselves' resource books provide a meticulously researched yet flexible structure for examining complex events and ideas. Educators can select appropriate readings and draw on additional resources available online or from our comprehensive lending library.

Our foundational resource book, *Facing History and Ourselves: Holocaust and Human Behavior*, embodies a sequence of study that begins with identity—first individual identity and then group and national identities, with their definitions of membership. From there the program examines the failure of democracy in Germany and the steps leading to the Holocaust—the most documented case of twentieth-century indifference, de-humanization, hatred, racism, antisemitism, and mass murder. It goes on to explore difficult questions of judgment, memory, and legacy, and the necessity for responsible participation to prevent injustice. Facing History and Ourselves then returns to the theme of civic participation to examine stories of individuals, groups, and nations who have worked to build just and inclusive communities and whose stories illuminate the courage, compassion, and political will that are needed to protect democracy today and in generations to come. Other examples in which civic dilemmas test democracy, such as the Armenian Genocide and the US civil rights movement, expand and deepen the connection between history and the choices we face today and in the future.

Facing History and Ourselves has offices or resource centers in the United States, Canada, and the United Kingdom as well as in-depth partnerships in Rwanda, South Africa, and Northern Ireland. Facing History and Ourselves' outreach is global, with educators trained in more than 80 countries and delivery of our resources through a website accessed worldwide with online content delivery, a program for international fellows, and a set of NGO partnerships. By convening conferences of scholars, theologians, educators, and journalists, Facing History and Ourselves' materials are kept timely, relevant, and responsive to salient issues of global citizenship in the twenty-first century.

For more than 30 years, Facing History and Ourselves has challenged students and educators to connect the complexities of the past to the moral and ethical issues of today. They explore democratic values and consider what it means to exercise one's rights and responsibilities in the service of a more humane and compassionate world. They become aware that "little things are big"—seemingly minor decisions can have a major impact and change the course of history.

For more about Facing History and Ourselves, visit our website at *www.facinghistory.org*.

ACKNOWLEDGMENTS

Primary writer: Elisabeth Fieldstone Kanner

Facing History and Ourselves extends much gratitude to the many individuals and groups whose thoughtful conversations, committed partnerships, and generous support made this project possible. We thank the Fledgling Fund for its generous support for the development of this study guide. Special recognition goes to Nicholas Kristof and *Reporter* filmmakers Eric Daniel Metzgar and Mikaela Beardsley for making an important, engaging film and for their contributions to this study guide.

We would also like to recognize our staff and others who contributed to the creation of this study guide: Our editorial team, Pamela Donaldson, Tanya Huellet, Mark Davis, Deb Chad, Adam Strom, Marc Skvirsky, Marty Sleeper, Dimitry Anselme, and Margot Stern Strom, reviewed numerous iterations of the manuscript. Rebecca Hamilton continues to be a wonderful friend to Facing History, sharing with us her experience as a reporter and an anti-genocide activist. Elisabeth Fieldstone Kanner synthesized comments from many sources to create this valuable study guide. April Lambert and Catherine O'Keefe oversaw the production of this study guide with wisdom, energy, and efficiency. Emma Smizik and Ronnie Millar coordinated our work, and our research intern Hilary Walker devoted countless hours to the project. We would also like to thank Sara Arnold for her copyediting, Tom Beckham for his work designing this guide, and Will Okun for supporting us in many aspects of this project, including graciously permitting us to use his photography throughout the guide.

TABLE OF CONTENTS

FILM SYNOPSIS 1

RATIONALE 2

SUGGESTIONS FOR USING THIS STUDY GUIDE 6

INTRODUCING *REPORTER* 8
    Pre-Viewing Reading 1: Letter to Students from Nicholas Kristof 8
    Pre-Viewing Reading 2: Leana Wen's Winning Essay 9
    Pre-Viewing Reading 3: Will Okun's Winning Essay 10

VIEWING GUIDE FOR *REPORTER* 11
    Pre-Viewing Questions 11
    Viewing Questions 11
    Post-Viewing Questions 13

INVESTIGATION ONE: Why don't people act? Confronting psychic numbing 15
    Reading 1: "Save the Darfur Puppy" 17
    Reading 2: Psychic Numbing and Genocide 19

INVESTIGATION TWO: Should reporters advocate? Exploring the role of journalists 23
    Reading 3: "A Student, a Teacher and a Glimpse of War" 25
    Reading 4: *On the Media* 27

INVESTIGATION THREE: What do we learn from the news? How reporters' choices
shape our understanding of the world 32
    Reading 5: "Dinner with a Warlord" 35
    Reading 6: "Killing in the Name of God" 36
    Reading 7: "Fear" 37
    Reading 8: "3-Way Battles Again Jolt Eastern Congo" 39
    Reading 9: Images of Congo 40

INVESTIGATION FOUR: What can we do to help? Education and action 45
    Reading 10: "What Can We Do to Help?" 46

WEB RESOURCES FOR *REPORTER* 50

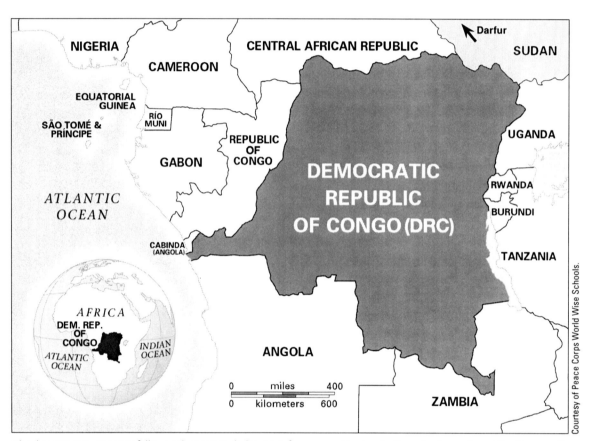

The documentary *Reporter* follows columnist Nicholas Kristof on a reporting trip to Rwanda, Burundi, and the Democratic Republic of Congo (DRC). The DRC, formerly Zaire, is often referred to as Congo, and should not confused with the Republic of Congo, its neighbor to the west. The film also makes references to Kristof's work in Darfur, a western region in Sudan.

REPORTER: FILM SYNOPSIS

Directed, edited, and photographed by Eric Daniel Metzgar
Produced by Mikaela Beardsley and Steven Cantor
Executive Producer: Ben Affleck
Running time: 90 minutes

Reporter is a feature documentary about Nicholas Kristof, a two-time Pulitzer Prize–winning columnist for the *New York Times*. In the summer of 2007, Kristof traveled to the Democratic Republic of Congo to shine his light into the darkest pockets of conflict and poverty. Congo is a country in the midst of a humanitarian crisis. To date, 5.4 million people have been killed in Congo over the last decade. Kristof's charge is to put Congo on the international agenda. To help attract a broader audience, Kristof invited a college student and a teacher—winners of the 2007 "Win a Trip with Nick" contest—to join him on this reporting trip to central Africa.

Reporter gives us access to the dilemmas Kristof confronts as a journalist who has an agenda: to get his audience to care and take action. Kristof knows that statistics deaden his readers' interest and compassion. To get the world to care, he goes in search of individuals whose stories will reflect the country's desperate crisis, including a dying woman, a rebel militia leader, and a child soldier.

From left to right: photographer and teacher Will Okun, medical student Leana Wen, *New York Times* columnist Nick Kristof, and filmmaker Eric Daniel Metzgar.

RATIONALE

In the documentary *Reporter*, we follow *New York Times* columnist Nicholas Kristof as he works to get his readers to "care about what happens on the other side of the hill." We see how he uses social science research and the tools of journalism to try to expand his readers' universe of responsibility—the people whom they feel obligated to care for and protect. We watch him struggle with dilemmas: How can he inform people about the larger context of genocide and other humanitarian disasters without numbing his readers' sense of compassion? As a print journalist, how can he adapt to the changing landscape of web-based media? What is the relationship between journalism and advocacy?

For over thirty years, Facing History and Ourselves has asked the same questions that underlie Kristof's work: Under what conditions do people care about others? When does that care translate into thoughtful action? What are the responsibilities of citizens to participate in their communities—local, national, and global? How can information be used and abused? By raising questions about the role of the reporter and the responsibility of the citizen, this documentary supports Facing History's mission to encourage students, educators, and community members to reflect on the types of civic engagement required by a vibrant democracy. While Kristof uses the tools of journalism, Facing History uses the tools of history and the humanities to help students, educators, and community members understand the conditions that encourage us to act (or to stand by) in the face of injustice, hatred, and mass violence. The resources we publish and the professional development Facing History provides follow a sequence of study—what Facing History calls its scope and sequence—that helps us wrestle with questions of identity, membership, decision-making, justice, and civic participation.*

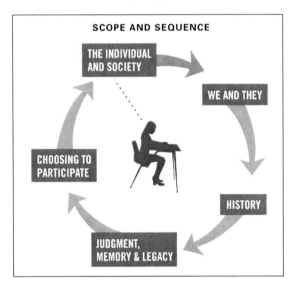

This documentary aligns with Facing History's scope and sequence by contributing to the study of history. For example, when investigating examples of injustice, such as the Holocaust or apartheid-era South Africa, students often ask, "How could this have happened?" Watching *Reporter* provides us with tools we can use to confront this question, such as social science research explaining the "psychology of compassion." By raising questions about the role of the media to intervene in stopping the genocide in Darfur or preventing violence against women in the Democratic Republic of Congo**, *Reporter*

---

* To learn more about Facing History's approach, refer to the preface and introduction in the resource book *Facing History and Ourselves: Holocaust and Human Behavior* (http://www.facinghistory.org/resources/hhb).

** The Democratic Republic of Congo (DRC), formerly Zaire, is often referred to as Congo by Nicholas Kristof and by other characters in *Reporter*. To maintain consistency, in this guide we also refer to the DRC as Congo. To avoid confusing the DRC with the Republic of Congo, its neighbor to the west, we suggest reviewing a map of Africa, such as the one at the beginning of this guide, which clearly differentiates between these two nations.

invites us to consider the role of the press during times throughout history when human rights have been abused.

Reporter also contributes to the final stage of Facing History's scope and sequence—"choosing to participate"—which focuses on stories of individuals and groups who have tried to make a positive impact on society. By studying these examples, we begin to answer the question, "What factors encourage us to take a stand on behalf of ourselves and others?" Investigation One of this study guide explores how Kristof confronts this question in *Reporter* as he struggles to get his readers to care about the genocide in Darfur and the humanitarian crisis in Congo.*

Is it the role of the reporter to inspire people to care? Should journalists try to guide their readers toward particular actions? Or is the reporter's job limited to providing accurate information? Investigation Two examines these questions. Kristof believes in the power of journalism to galvanize people to solve the world's problems. For example, he has worked tirelessly to bring attention to the genocide in Darfur. In *Reporter*, we hear actress and activist Mia Farrow** explain, "It was Nick [who] sounded the clarion call. That there was a genocide unfolding in a place called Darfur. . . . It was through reading Nick's columns that I [gained] knowledge of a situation in a place I never heard of." Samantha Power, author of *A Problem from Hell: America and the Age of Genocide*, describes Kristof's efforts as "relentless":

> He would find a hundred different angles into the same subject, but the central message was consistent and, in its own way, repetitive. Genocide is happening and you're not doing enough to stop it. Moreover, you have the power to stop it, and that makes you doubly responsible.[1]

For his work writing about the genocide in Darfur, Kristof was awarded a Pulitzer Prize. While much of his work focuses on problems facing people in Asia and Africa, in his column he also draws attention to domestic issues, including heath care, poverty, and education. Most recently, Kristof and his wife, journalist Sheryl WuDunn, wrote a book about the plight of women around the world called *Half the Sky: Turning Oppression into Opportunity for Women Worldwide*.† According to Kristof, they wrote *Half the Sky* "not so much to inform people as because we wanted to shake people up and help address these issues."[2]

Nicholas Kristof follows a long line of journalists who have used their role to advocate for action and change. For decades, Ida B. Wells†† used journalism "as a weapon against racial bigotry."[3] While

---

* Decades before Kristof's outrage over the international community's inability to stop the genocide in Darfur, Raphael Lemkin expressed outrage over the world's response, or lack thereof, to the Armenian genocide during World War I. Lemkin's frustration led him to coin the term "genocide." For more information about the meaning of genocide and Lemkin's struggle to have this concept recognized in international law, refer to our study guide *Totally Unofficial: Raphael Lemkin and the Genocide Convention* (http://www.facinghistory.org/resources/publications/lemkin).

** Mia Farrow has been a United Nations Goodwill Ambassador since 2000. In 2008, *Time* magazine named her one of the most influential people in the world, highlighting her work to end the genocide in Darfur.

† The website http://www.halftheskymovement.org, a companion to the book *Half the Sky*, provides information about women around the world and what can be done to improve their situations for the benefit of all.

†† Chapter 2, "The Promise of American Democracy," in the first edition of *Facing History and Ourselves: Choosing to Participate* (http://www.facinghistory.org/resources/publications/facing-history-choosing-participate) includes a case study on Ida B. Wells.

best known for her articles exposing the injustices of lynching, she also wrote against Jim Crow segregation and in support of women's suffrage. During World War I, journalists' accounts of the mass murder of Armenians rallied the public to pressure their governments to intervene and stop the abuses. Americans reacted to these reports of suffering Armenians with one of the largest humanitarian responses in the history of the United States.[4] Throughout the civil rights movement, some journalists recognized the role that the press had in furthering the cause against racial discrimination and even risked their lives to report on the civil rights struggle.[5]

During the civil rights movement, "the press" meant newspapers, magazines, and television. In the Internet age, the media world is far more complicated. Kristof and others refer to this changing media landscape throughout *Reporter*. For anyone with a cell phone or a computer, technology presents exciting opportunities to disseminate their ideas to a public audience. As a result, never before have we had as much access to information from so many sources. Acknowledging that we are living in the "most informed of times," scholar Vartan Gregorian* wonders, "How can all of this knowledge add up to real understanding?"[6] Today, comprehending the words on the page or in a broadcast is no longer sufficient; we need to be able interpret media with regard to the purpose and perspective of its creators. Investigation Three of this study guide includes six different accounts of Congo published around the same time. Comparing these texts gives us the opportunity to practice the media literacy skills that Professor Pat Aufderheide says are "a basic tool for citizenship in an Information Society."[7]

> "The people must know before they can act..."
> — Ida B. Wells

Ultimately, the consequences of reporting are decided not by the journalists but by the audience. Ida B. Wells wrote hundreds of articles about lynching, but this dreadful practice continued well beyond her death. Kristof wrote dozens of columns about Darfur, yet over a million Darfuris are living in refugee camps, unable to return to their homes. Why is this? Eric Metzgar, the director of *Reporter*, provides one answer: "Nick won his second Pulitzer Prize for helping to put the Darfur crisis on the international radar. But the violence continues because it's not enough for the public to simply know about a calamity; we have to care."[8] And for change to take place, we also have to act based on that caring.

But is it the reporter's role to tell us how to act? No, it is not, according to Metzgar. He argues:

> In terms of human rights issues, I don't believe in this kind of obedient action-taking, if you will.... If you need to be told what to do, I don't think that that equals the sustained compassion that is required for us to really take on these issues. You know, if you really want to know what to do, [it] takes five seconds to put "Congo crisis help" into a Google search engine and then you're off. There are a million things you can do. If I tell you one thing that I would do, that directs everyone down one path. You know, you have to figure out what moves you the most and take your own path.[9]

---

* Vartan Gregorian has spent his life advancing the use of knowledge for human progress and public service. Prior to assuming his current role as president of the Carnegie Corporation of New York, he worked in universities around the country as a professor, dean, provost, and president. He was also president of the New York Public Library.

Once you have identified what "moves you the most," what can you do to help? In particular, how can media—new and old—be used as a tool to prevent injustice and violence, and also as a tool to encourage people to respond when children, women, and men are suffering? This is the question explored in Investigation Four of this study guide.

Watching *Reporter* and using the materials in this study guide encourage us to consider how the changing landscape of journalism expands and complicates our role as creators and consumers of the news. We live in a time when technology gives each of us the opportunity to serve as reporter. What opportunities and challenges does the "democratization of media" present? How will our choices as consumers of media shape our understanding of the world? How will our choices as creators of media shape our communities, near and far?

---

1. *Reporter*, (00:12:25).

2. Kristi Heim, "Half the Sky: Q&A with Nicholas Kristof," *The Seattle Times*, October 9, 2009, *http://seattletimes.nwsource.com/html/thebusinessofgiving/2010032989_questions_for_nicholas_kristof.html.*

3. Pamela Newkirk, "Ida B. Wells-Barnett: Journalism as a Weapon Against Racial Bigotry," *Media Studies Journal* 14 (Spring/Summer 2000), accessed August 13, 2010, *http://www.hartford-hwp.com/archives/45a/317.html.*

4. Facing History and Ourselves, *Crime Against Humanity: The Genocide of the Armenians* (Brookline, MA: Facing History and Ourselves National Foundation, Inc., 2004), 134–141.

5. Jack Nelson, "The Civil Rights Movement: A Press Perspective," *Human Rights Magazine* (Fall 2001), *http://www.abanet.org/irr/hr/fall01/nelson.html.*

6. Vartan Gregorian, foreword in *Public Scholarship: A New Perspective for the 21st Century*, a report by the Carnegie Corporation of New York (2004), 5.

7. "Media Literacy Definitions & Quotes," *http://www.frankwbaker.com/Media_Lit_Quotes.html.*

8. "Transcript: Caring About Congo," *NOW on PBS*, February 12, 2010, *http://www.pbs.org/now/shows/607/transcript.html.*

9. Ibid.

SUGGESTIONS FOR USING THIS STUDY GUIDE

This study guide has been designed to be used with the documentary *Reporter*, produced by Stick Figure Productions. There are many ways to engage with the film and the materials in this study guide. Some teachers will show the entire 90-minute documentary and have students explore one or more of the investigations included in this guide. Other classrooms might watch an excerpt from *Reporter* and focus on one or two questions from the Viewing Guide. Regardless of how students explore these materials, we recommend following a similar path:

1. Prepare students to view *Reporter*: Before viewing all or part of *Reporter*, prepare students for the ideas and themes they are about to explore. You might have students write about and/or discuss one of the Pre-Viewing Questions in the Viewing Guide. Or, to help students think about the purpose for making (and watching) *Reporter*, you could have them read the letter from Nicholas Kristof or excerpts from Leana Wen and Will Okun's "Win a Trip with Nick" winning essays (see pages 9–10). On page 50, we have included links to resources that describe the humanitarian conflicts referred to in the film—civil war in Congo and the genocide in Darfur. Prior to watching *Reporter*, reviewing the background for these conflicts can increase students' engagement and comprehension of this material. Additional pre-viewing lesson ideas can be found on our *Reporter* website (*reporter.facinghistory.org*).

2. View all or part of *Reporter*: While watching the film, we suggest pausing at key moments to clarify understanding and to give students the opportunity to respond in writing or discussion to what they have viewed. For ideas on when you might stop the film, consult the Viewing Guide. It includes time codes for suggested pause moments related to specific questions about themes raised in this film. If you only have time to show a part of *Reporter*, reviewing the investigation overviews can help you select film excerpts that address themes and questions most appropriate for your learning objectives.

3. Reflect on questions and ideas raised in *Reporter*: Listening to students' reactions—noting their interests, questions, and misconceptions—will inform your decisions about how to debrief after their viewing of *Reporter*. Exploring one or more of the investigations is a useful post-viewing exercise. The lesson ideas on the *Reporter* website (*reporter.facinghistory.org*) suggest different ways to use the readings in the investigations to deepen students' understanding of the ideas addressed in the film. The lesson ideas also recommend projects and assignments that can be used to evaluate students' learning.

Educational resources in the study guide

- **Pre-Viewing Readings:** To prepare students to view all or part of *Reporter*, we have included three readings that introduce students to the main characters in the documentary: Nicholas Kristof, Leana Wen, and Will Okun. Their writings foreshadow many of the important themes and questions raised by the film.
- **Viewing Guide:** The Viewing Guide includes Pre-Viewing Questions, Viewing Questions, and Post-Viewing Questions. These questions explore the film's specific content as it relates to universal themes such as empathy, social responsibility, and perspective-taking. They can be used to facilitate large- and small-group discussions, prompt reflective writing, develop projects, and evaluate student understanding. Questions are labeled with time codes from the film to allow you to select specific moments on which to focus.
- **Investigations:** To deepen students' understanding of key themes in the film, ten supplementary readings have been included in this study guide. Readings are organized into four investigations that correspond to specific excerpts and themes from the film. (Refer to the table of contents for a list of readings by investigation.) Each investigation includes the following parts:
  - **Overviews:** Overviews frame the readings and explain how they connect to an excerpt of the film.
  - **Readings:** Many of the readings included in the study guide—editorials, blog entries, and photographs—were created by Nicholas Kristof, Leana Wen, and Will Okun while they were on the trip that is the subject of this documentary. We have also identified additional readings, such as an excerpt from Paul Slovic's study on psychic numbing, to give students an opportunity to further explore ideas presented in *Reporter*. We strongly recommend that you preview readings to judge if the content and reading level are appropriate for your students. Acknowledging that some readings may be challenging for students, on our website we have posted teaching strategies aimed at helping students comprehend and interpret challenging text (*www.facinghistory.org/teachingstrategies*).
  - **Connections:** After the readings, you will find a collection of questions selected to help clarify and deepen students' understanding of themes raised in each investigation. They bring up points of view that are not represented in the readings and provide opportunities for students to connect the ideas in the texts to their own experiences. Teachers often select one or two questions as the focus for class discussion, journal writing, or an assessment activity. Sometimes teachers allow students to write about or discuss the question most interesting to them.
- **Web Resources for *Reporter*:** We have identified helpful online resources that provide background on events in the Democratic Republic of Congo and Darfur. We also suggest websites that provide information about Nicholas Kristof, journalism, and writing a news story. As a pre-viewing resource, information from these links provides students with context to help them understand the material in the film. As a post-viewing resource, information from these sites can help students continue their exploration of questions and themes raised in the film.

In addition to these resources, Facing History has developed a website, *reporter.facinghistory.org*, that includes streaming video, lesson ideas, and other educational materials for *Reporter*.

INTRODUCING *REPORTER*: PRE-VIEWING READINGS

The following readings help prepare students to watch *Reporter* and explore the materials in this study guide.

Pre-Viewing Reading 1: Letter to Students from Nicholas Kristof

The film *Reporter* follows *New York Times* columnist Nicholas Kristof on a reporting trip to central Africa. Facing History asked Kristof what he hoped students would learn from watching *Reporter*, and he responded with the following letter. What message do you take away from this letter? What does this note reveal about Kristof's goals as a journalist? How would you respond to him?

Dear student,

Watching *Reporter* and reading materials from its study guide, you probably won't want to come to dinner with me—at least not if a warlord is joining us. But I hope you'll be nourished, if not by a meal together, at least by the ideas in here. Frankly, these are tough issues for high-school students, or for people of any age, and some readers might think that they are more appropriate only for university students. War, genocide and rape are evils we naturally turn away from. But I hope you will not only recognize the horrors of these conflicts, but also appreciate that they are not inevitable. We can make a difference, we can chip away at these kinds of outrages, and we can as a result make this a somewhat better world. And since these brutalities are happening to kids your age, and those much younger—often by perpetrators who are also your age or younger—it's hard to argue that they are irrelevant to your age group. So welcome to this journey, and I invite you to feel not only outrage but also a sense that you can give voice to the voiceless.

Nicholas Kristof

Nicholas Kristof, two-time Pulitzer Prize winner and *New York Times* columnist since 2001, has written extensively about human rights abuses across the world, from Darfur to Indonesia.

8 *TEACHING* **REPORTER**

"Win a Trip With Nick" Winning Essays (April 29, 2007)

In 2007, *New York Times* columnist Nicholas Kristof invited teachers and college students to apply to "Win a Trip with Nick." Medical student Leana Wen and Chicago teacher Will Okun wrote the winning essays that gave them the opportunity to join Kristof on a reporting trip to central Africa that summer. *Reporter* tells the story of their trip. Below, we have included excerpts from Wen and Okun's winning essays. What do these texts reveal about the winners' reasons for taking this trip? Why do you think Kristof asked a teacher and a college student to join him?

Pre-Viewing Reading 2: Leana Wen's Winning Essay[1] (excerpt)

If we just looked for them, we can find injustices everywhere. Hurricane Katrina exposed Americans to abject poverty and health disparities right in our backyard. Many more injustices exist "over there," in developing nations, that result in millions of preventable deaths and lifetimes of wasted talent and squandered opportunity. I want to fight these injustices and change the world.

My upbringing exposed me to injustices firsthand. Raised in a dissident family in China, I came to the US on political asylum after the Tiananmen Square massacre. We were outsiders in a Communist regime and remained outsiders in predominantly Mormon Utah and then inner-city Los Angeles. Though Shanghai, Logan, and Compton have little else in common, they all bear witness to the differences between the haves and have-nots, and I grew up keenly aware of the impact of political, cultural, and socioeconomic oppression.

Since graduating from medical school, Leana Wen has practiced emergency medicine in the United States and traveled around the world speaking about global health issues.

As a child with life-threatening asthma and debilitating speech impediment, I also confronted the stigma of disability and the challenges of seeking health care with limited resources.

Yet the mechanisms to address injustices eluded me. I thought that becoming a doctor would allow me to help those most in need; however, I witnessed more problems than found solutions that had sustainable rather than short-term impact. . . . Pills might help the individual patients at that point in their lives, but [that] does not resolve the root causes of their problems.

Global change requires more than pills and individual-level change: it hinges on concerted education and mobilization. . . . It is to learn communication to the public as a method of effecting change that I apply for this opportunity. . . . Treating a patient's problems and moving on to the next ailment is not enough, and I want instead to convey my patients' stories and describe their communities' struggles. I want to solve global problems by educating and motivating the public to action. I want to learn these tools from you.

Pre-Viewing Reading 3: Will Okun's Winning Essay[2] (excerpt)

Nearly every day after school, I go to students' houses to shoot photographs of the students with their families and friends. Since our school, Westside Alternative High School, is located in one of the lowest-income communities of Chicago, there is ample opportunity to photograph the poverty which seemingly envelops their lives. . . . But I do not take these pictures. These pictures have already been taken. Book after book, exhibit upon exhibit depict only the poverty and misery of the current black community in America. Unless you happen to live or work in a black community, it is likely that blacks are perceived by the majority of America as either extremely poor and sad (from the media and photographs) or extremely materialistic and "gangsta" (from rap music and videos).

Will Okun taught English and photography for nine years at Westside Alternative High School in Chicago. His photography website, *www.wjzo.com*, features portraits of his former students and their families, as well as images from his trip to central Africa with Nicholas Kristof.

Instead, I seek to capture the happiness and joy that can occur in everyday moments and the beauty that exists within every person, regardless of their income. Most importantly, I try to produce unique portraits that capture the essence of each person. Secondly, I want the people to be happy with their own photographs. Nothing gives me greater satisfaction than going into a student's house and seeing my framed pictures on the walls. Lastly, I hope my photographs offer another perspective of black American teenagers that is largely inaccessible to the general public. (My photographs are posted on my *www.wjzo.com* website, which receives over 30,000 views a week from all over the world.)

This is the perspective I will bring to Africa with Nick Kristof. While America is only presented with images representative of Africa's poverty and misery, I will seek stories and photographs that will offer our young people a more comprehensive depiction of African people and culture. I hope my photographs and stories will present young Africans with an opportunity to educate, communicate with, and relate to young Americans. In addition, I hope to produce photographs and stories that will emote pleasure and pride from the Africans themselves.

---

1. Leana Wen, "Winning Essay: Leana Wen," *New York Times,* April 29, 2007, accessed September 19, 2010, http://www.nytimes.com/2007/04/29/opinion/29wat-wen.html.

2. Will Okun, "Winning Essay: Will Okun," *New York Times,* April 29, 2007, accessed September 19, 2010, http://www.nytimes.com/2007/04/29/opinion/29wat-okun.html.

VIEWING GUIDE FOR *REPORTER*

The following questions can be used to facilitate large- and small-group discussions, prompt reflective writing, develop projects, and evaluate student understanding. They are meant to complement, not replace, the questions raised by students themselves. Also, keep in mind that after exposure to new material, the best questions are often the simplest: What have you just seen? What ideas strike you as important or interesting? What questions does this material raise for you? What perspectives were represented? Which perspectives were left out or de-emphasized?

Pre-Viewing Questions

1. Mother Teresa, a nun famous for her work helping the poor, said, "If I look at the mass, I will never act. If I look at the one, I will." What do you think Mother Teresa meant by this statement? Do you agree or disagree with her? Explain.

2. What is "the news"? Describe your habits related to the news. Where do you get the news? How often do you read, watch, or listen to the news? What stories interest you the most? Identify a news story you heard recently that got your attention. What about this story engaged you?

3. Write a job description for a reporter. What is a reporter's job? What skills are required to do this job well?

4. If you wanted to get people to care about an issue facing your community, how would you get them to care? What information would be most likely to motivate people to do something to address this issue?

5. What do you know about the Democratic Republic of Congo? How or where did you learn this information? What do you know about Darfur? How or where did you learn this information?

Viewing Questions

(Time codes indicate where you might pause the film to reflect on the question in writing or through discussion.)

1. Who is Nicholas Kristof? What do we know about him? (6:30)

2. Journalism expert Tom Rosenstiel believes that travel is important to Kristof's work as a reporter, explaining, "I think that bearing witness is a critical element of what makes some columns better than others, and there are certain kinds of stories that need to have witness borne in person. It just is more powerful to go there." What does it mean to "bear witness"? What responsibilities come with bearing witness to an event or situation? (7:16)

VIEWING GUIDE 11

3. Stephen Colbert asks Kristof, "Why should we pay attention to the rest of the world?" How would you respond to this question? (14:03)

4. Describe the results of the Rokia study. What did Paul Slovic learn about the "psychology of compassion" from this study? To what degree do these results represent your own experience? (16:31)

5. In the film, Kristof says, "I'm outraged at what I see and I want it to stop, and I think one way you can fight a militia is with UN peacekeepers with large guns. Another way you can fight them is with small notebooks and pens." Respond to Kristof's statement. To what extent can a journalist help stop civil war and prevent human rights abuses, if at all? (22:40)

6. Describing his dilemma about whether or not to travel to a displacement camp outside of Goma, Kristof explains, "I want to get a good story but I don't want to put them [Leana and Will] at risk or make them feel uncomfortable." What are the risks involved in this mission? What advice would you give to Kristof as he decides whether to go or turn back? What do you think he will decide to do? What makes you think this? (30:54)

7. Kristof reveals that most of the time when he hears stories of rape and abuse, they don't really bother him because he approaches these stories with "professional distance." How do you reconcile (make sense of) Kristof's desire to rouse compassion in his readers and his own dispassionate (unemotional) reaction to these stories? Is compassion something that can be turned on and off like a switch? If so, what activates our sense of empathy? What turns it off? (36:25)

8. What is the difference between the way Leana Wen responds to Yohanita and the way Nicholas Kristof responds? Given that their purpose for being in this village is to find a story, do you think that the team of journalists should stop their reporting to try to save Yohanita? Why or why not? (55:14)

9. How does General Nkunda explain how he came to have his position as leader of a rebel militia? He calls himself a "liberator," while Kristof refers to him as a "warlord." Which title is most appropriate for him? What does this exchange reveal about the power of language? (1:13:27)

10. What are your thoughts after seeing Kristof interview child soldiers? What did the child soldiers do to end up as Nkunda's prisoners? If they are guilty of committing crimes, should they be punished for their actions even though they are under the age of 18? Should we think of the actions of child soldiers the same way we think about the actions of adult soldiers? Why or why not? (1:15:56)

11. At the end of the film, the narrator says, "The most recent statistic states that 5.4 million people have died in Congo over the last decade as a result of the ongoing warfare, and that 1.2 million people are now displaced in eastern Congo alone." What does Kristof think needs to happen to end the humanitarian disaster in Congo? Who do you think is responsible for helping the Congolese? (1:28:15)

Post-Viewing Questions

1. Identify an image from the film that was particularly powerful for you. What about this image moved you? How did it make you feel? What questions does it raise for you?

2. Why do you think the filmmakers made this film? What message (or messages) are they trying to express? What do you notice about how the filmmakers shot the film? What techniques did they use to help communicate their message? What might you have done differently if you were the filmmaker?

3. Why do you think Kristof wanted to bring a college student and a teacher with him on a reporting trip to central Africa? Why bring a student and a teacher, as opposed to anyone in the general public? What do you think of this decision? Would you want to travel with Kristof on a reporting trip? Why or why not?

4. Kristof argues that the media does not pay enough attention to the problems in Congo and other places around the world. Yet some people criticize him for only covering stories that involve human misery (wars, disease, extreme poverty, etc.). What do you think of this critique of Kristof's writing? Is his coverage unfair to Congo? Why or why not?

5. Kristof assumes that it is important for people to know about what is happening "on the other side of the hill." Yet most of us only have a limited amount of time to read or watch the news. Where do you think our attention should be focused—on learning about places close to home or far away, or both? Explain your answer.

6. Nicholas Kristof is a columnist whose articles appear on an editorial page. His articles do not appear in the news section of the paper. Does this distinction matter? Why or why not?

7. Identify a challenge or dilemma Kristof confronts when writing his column. What do you think about how he handles this situation?

8. Describe Kristof's method for writing his column. What do you think of his writing method? What aspects of it appeal to you? What aspects of it concern you? What tips about reporting do you take away from watching *Reporter*?

9. Kristof explains, "I spent a lot of time trying to put various crises on the international map. Maybe the most difficult to put there is Congo." What has made it so hard to bring attention to the devastation in Congo? What does this reveal about the way that news is reported and published? Would you suggest any changes to the criteria that get a story on the front page? If so, what would they be?

10. Kristof hopes that his writing galvanizes people to do something to make the world a better place. Has reading a newspaper article or editorial ever roused you to take action? If so, why do you think this article affected you? If not, why do you think this is the case? What has inspired you to care about others?

11. When you feel an obligation to care for and protect someone, you include that person in your universe of responsibility. Who does Kristof include in his universe of responsibility? What do you know about Kristof's identity—his values, background, and experiences—that might have influenced how he defines his universe of responsibility? Who do you include in your universe of responsibility? What has influenced your choices about whom to include?

INVESTIGATION ONE
Why don't people act? Confronting psychic numbing

The readings in this investigation have been selected to deepen our understanding of ideas presented in chapters 3 and 4 (12:05–19:56) of the documentary *Reporter* (approximately 8 minutes). In this clip, Stephen Colbert asks his guest on *The Colbert Report*, Nicholas Kristof, "Why should we pay attention to the rest of the world?" Kristof answers this question by referring to social science research about "the psychology of compassion" and explains how he applies this knowledge when writing about the genocide in Darfur.

Overview

According to the International Association of Genocide Scholars, in the twentieth century more people have died from genocide and mass murder than from all wars.[1] After each atrocity, men and women in the international community cry "Never again," but human rights abuses against innocent children, women, and men continue. In his job as a reporter for the *New York Times*, Nicholas Kristof has been able to see these human rights abuses firsthand, winning a Pulitzer Prize for bringing attention to the genocide in Darfur. Yet despite the attention Kristof and others have drawn to this humanitarian disaster, the violence continues. Why is this the case?

Looking to history can help us address this question. In the 1940s, Jan Karski, a courier for the Polish resistance, publicized reports about Nazi atrocities to a mostly unbelieving audience. After the war, he spoke of his attempts to alert people to the mass murder of European Jews, explaining, "The tragedy was that these testimonies were not believed. Not because of ill will, but simply because the facts were beyond human imagination."[2] During the Holocaust, many people did not intervene to stop the genocide because they were not able to "imagine the unimaginable." As Professor Larry Langer argues, "Even with the evidence before our eyes, we hesitate to accept the worst."[*]

In his editorial "Save the Darfur Puppy," Kristof provides another reason why many people do not respond when confronted with information about genocide or humanitarian disasters. Drawing on the work of Paul Slovic, a professor who studies the psychology of compassion, Kristof explains that "the human conscience just isn't pricked by mass suffering, while an individual child (or puppy) in distress causes our hearts to flutter."[3] He refers to studies that demonstrate how people are more likely to help one person, or even one animal, than they are to help hundreds of suffering people. This investigation includes that editorial as well as an excerpt from the abstract[**] of Slovic's study on psychic numbing and genocide.

---

[*] The reading "Is Knowledge Enough?" (pages 367–370) in *Facing History and Ourselves: Holocaust and Human Behavior* provides more information about why people may have ignored or discounted information about Nazi atrocities during the Holocaust.

[**] An abstract is a brief summary that highlights the main points of an academic study.

Both of these readings help us think about a concept called "psychic numbing." Psychiatrist Robert J. Lifton* coined this term to refer to "a general category of diminished capacity or inclination to feel."[4] Writing about the "numbing of everyday life," he explains, "We are bombarded by all kinds of images and influences and we have to fend some of them off if we're to take in any of them, or to carry through just our ordinary day's work. . . ."[5] In her book *High Tide in Tucson*, novelist Barbara Kingsolver affirms Lifton's observation that people numb themselves to disturbing information:

> Confronted with knowledge of dozens of apparently random disasters each day, what can a human heart do but slam its doors? No mortal can grieve that much. We didn't evolve to cope with tragedy on a global scale. Our defense is to pretend there's no thread of event that connects us, and that those lives are somehow not precious and real like our own. It's a practical strategy, to some ends, but the loss of empathy is also the loss of humanity, and that's no small tradeoff.[6]

Kingsolver writes about how the loss of empathy is also the loss of humanity: by closing themselves off to caring for others, people can allow horrible crimes to occur.

> "It is possible to live in a twilight between knowing and not knowing.
> It is possible to refuse full realization of facts because one feels
> unable to face the implications of these facts."[7]
> — W. A. Visser't Hooft, a Dutch theologian, explaining why he and many others
> discounted early accounts of Nazi crimes

While acknowledging the costs of psychic numbing, Lifton also identifies a benefit: sometimes numbing allows you to perform a task that would be challenging if you were distracted by strong emotions. He explains:

> And yet, [psychic numbing] isn't all negative. For instance, I realize that if you take the example of a surgeon who is performing a delicate operation, you don't want him or her to have the same emotions as a family member of that person being operated on. There has to be some level of detachment where you bring your technical skill to bear on it.[8]

Supporting Lifton's argument, Kristof reveals how he experiences a degree of psychic numbing in his own work as a journalist:

> In a career [of] reporting I heard a lot of really wrenching stories about murder and rape and everything else, and at this point, and see I'm not really proud of it, I may be a little embarrassed about it, [but] I can listen pretty dispassionately to the most inhuman stories. And they, most of the time, don't, you know, really bother me. Maybe it's that sort of clinical role of a—of a surgeon somewhere in [an] operating theater, but I can, you know, approach things normally as a journalist and treat it with a certain amount of professional distance.[9]

---

* Lifton found evidence of psychic numbing in the survivors of the atomic bomb at Hiroshima and in Nazi doctors who performed inhumane experiments on concentration camp prisoners.

While on the one hand Kristof describes how he approaches his work writing about human suffering "with a certain amount of professional distance," on the other hand he is bothered by these stories. While working in Cambodia, he was so affected by the plight of two young girls that he bought their freedom from a brothel.

Kristof's dilemma—how to express compassion for the people he meets while also writing the most effective story—represents a dilemma many of us confront. We live in an era of endless access to information about human suffering around the world. What do we do with this information? What should we do with it? There are no simple answers to these questions, and in our attempts to address them we confront how we define our universe of responsibility—the individuals and groups whom we feel an obligation to care for and protect. For whom do we show compassion and empathy? Why? Under what conditions? In the following readings, Kristof and Slovic point out that all too often we define our universe of responsibility narrowly, making room for only one person. What would our communities—local, national, and global—look like if more people were in the habit of paying attention to those in need, rather than tuning them out?

Reading 1: "Save the Darfur Puppy"[10]

The following editorial was written by columnist Nicholas Kristof and published in the *New York Times* opinion section on May 10, 2007.

NICHOLAS D. KRISTOF
Save the Darfur Puppy

Finally, we're beginning to understand what it would take to galvanize President Bush, other leaders and the American public to respond to the genocide in Sudan: a suffering puppy with big eyes and floppy ears.

That's the implication of a series of studies by psychologists trying to understand why people — good, conscientious people — aren't moved by genocide or famines. Time and again, we've seen that the human conscience just isn't pricked by mass suffering, while an individual child (or puppy) in distress causes our hearts to flutter.

In one experiment, psychologists asked ordinary citizens to contribute $5 to alleviate hunger abroad. In one version, the money would go to a particular girl, Rokia, a 7-year-old in Mali; in another, to 21 million hungry Africans; in a third, to Rokia — but she was presented as a victim of a larger tapestry of global hunger.

Not surprisingly, people were less likely to give to anonymous millions than to Rokia. But they were also less willing to give in the third scenario, in which Rokia's suffering was presented as part of a broader pattern.

Evidence is overwhelming that humans respond to the suffering of individuals rather than groups. Think of the toddler Jessica McClure falling down a well in 1987, or the Lindbergh baby kidnapping in 1932 (which Mencken described as the "the biggest story since the Resurrection").

Even the right animal evokes a similar sympathy. A dog stranded on a ship aroused so much pity that $48,000 in private money was spent trying to rescue it — and that was before the Coast Guard stepped in. And after I began visiting Darfur in 2004, I was flummoxed by the public's passion to save a red-tailed hawk, Pale

Reading continues on next page.

Male, that had been evicted from his nest on Fifth Avenue in New York City. A single homeless hawk aroused more indignation than two million homeless Sudanese.

Advocates for the poor often note that 30,000 children die daily of the consequences of poverty — presuming that this number will shock people into action. But the opposite is true: the more victims, the less compassion.

In one experiment, people in one group could donate to a $300,000 fund for medical treatments that would save the life of one child — or, in another group, the lives of eight children. People donated more than twice as much money to help save one child as to help save eight.

Likewise, remember how people were asked to save Rokia from starvation? A follow-up allowed students to donate to Rokia or to a hungry boy named Moussa. Both Rokia and Moussa attracted donations in the same proportions. Then another group was asked to donate to Rokia and Moussa together. But donors felt less good about supporting two children, and contributions dropped off.

"Our capacity to feel is limited," Paul Slovic of the University of Oregon writes in a new journal article, "Psychic Numbing and Genocide," which discusses these experiments. Professor Slovic argues that we cannot depend on the innate morality even of good people. Instead, he believes, we need to develop legal or political mechanisms to force our hands to confront genocide.

So, yes, we should develop early-warning systems for genocide, prepare an African Union, U.N. and NATO rapid-response capability, and polish the "responsibility to protect" as a legal basis to stop atrocities. (The Genocide Intervention Network and the Enough project are working on these things.)

But, frankly, after four years of watching the U.N. Security Council, the International Criminal Court and the Genocide Convention accomplish little in Darfur, I'm skeptical that either human rationality or international law can achieve much unless backed by a public outcry.

One experiment underscored the limits of rationality. People prepared to donate to the needy were first asked either to talk about babies (to prime the emotions) or to perform math calculations (to prime their rational side). Those who did math donated less.

So maybe what we need isn't better laws but more troubled consciences — pricked, perhaps, by a Darfur puppy with big eyes and floppy ears. Once we find such a soulful dog in peril, we should call ABC News. ABC's news judgment can be assessed by the 11 minutes of evening news coverage it gave to Darfur's genocide during all of last year — compared with 23 minutes for the false confession in the JonBenet Ramsey case.

If President Bush and the global public alike are unmoved by the slaughter of hundreds of thousands of fellow humans, maybe our last, best hope is that we can be galvanized by a puppy in distress. □

The "Rokia study" demonstrates that when people are shown a single human face, they are more likely to donate than when they are presented with statistics or even the image of two victims.

Reading 2: Psychic Numbing and Genocide[11]

The following excerpt is from the abstract (summary) of a research paper written by Dr. Paul Slovic, professor of psychology at the University of Oregon. It was published in the academic journal *Judgment and Decision Making* (April 2007).

Most people are caring and will exert great effort to rescue individual victims whose needy plight comes to their attention. These same good people, however, often become numbly indifferent to the plight of individuals who are "one of many" in a much greater problem. Why does this occur? The answer to this question will help us answer a related question that is the topic of this paper: Why, over the past century, have good people repeatedly ignored mass murder and genocide?...

My search to identify a fundamental deficiency in human psychology that causes us to ignore mass murder and genocide has led to a theoretical framework that describes the importance of emotions and feelings in guiding decision making and behavior. Perhaps the most basic form of feeling is affect, the sense (not necessarily conscious) that something is good or bad. Affective responses occur rapidly and automatically—note how quickly you sense the feelings associated with the word "treasure" or the word "hate."... One last important psychological element in this story is attention. Just as feelings are necessary for motivating helping, attention is necessary for feelings.

The behavioral theories and data confirm what keen observers of human behavior have long known. Numerical representations of human lives do not necessarily convey the importance of those lives.... The numbers are important, and yet they are not everything. For whatever reasons, images often strike us more powerfully, more deeply than numbers. We seem unable to hold the emotions aroused by numbers for nearly as long as those of images. We quickly grow numb to the facts and the math. Images seem to be the key to conveying affect and meaning, though some imagery is more powerful than others.

Figure 1: Imagery and attention produce feelings that motivate helping behavior.

Probably the most important image to represent a human life is that of a single human face. Journalist Paul Neville writes about the need to probe beneath the statistics of joblessness, homelessness, mental illness, and poverty in his home state of Oregon, in order to discover the people behind the numbers—who they are, what they look like, how they sound, what they feel, what hopes and fears they harbor. He concludes: "I don't know when we became a nation of statistics. But I know that the path to becoming a nation—and a community—of people is remembering the faces behind the numbers" (Neville, 2004). . . .

Perhaps there is hope that vivid, personalized media coverage of genocide could motivate intervention. Perhaps. But again we should look to research to assess these possibilities. Numerous experiments have demonstrated the "identifiable victim effect" which is also so evident outside the laboratory. . . . Small, Loewenstein, and Slovic (2007) gave people leaving a psychological experiment the opportunity to contribute up to $5 of their earnings to Save the Children. The study consisted of three separate conditions: (1) identifiable victim [image], (2) statistical victims [facts], and (3) identifiable victim with statistical information [image + facts]. . . . Participants in each condition were told that "any money donated will go toward relieving the severe food crisis in southern Africa and Ethiopia." The donations in fact went to Save the Children, but they were earmarked specifically for Rokia in Conditions 1 and 3 and not specifically earmarked in Condition 2. The average donations are presented in Figure 2. Donations in response to the identified individual, Rokia, were far greater than donations in response to the statistical portrayal of the food crisis. Most important, however, and most discouraging, was the fact that coupling the statistical realities with Rokia's story significantly reduced the contributions to Rokia. . . .

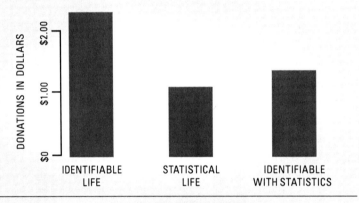

Figure 2: Mean donations when people are exposed to different information.[12]

Clearly there are political obstacles posing challenges to those who would consider intervention in genocide, and physical risks as well. What I have tried to describe in this paper are the formidable psychological obstacles centered around the difficulties in wrapping our minds around genocide and forming the emotional connections to its victims that are necessary to motivate us to overcome these other obstacles. . . . In this paper I have drawn upon common observation and behavioral research to argue that we cannot depend only upon our moral feelings to motivate us to take proper actions against genocide. That places the burden of response squarely upon the shoulders of moral argument and international law.

Connections

1. What is empathy? What is compassion? When have you felt empathy and/or compassion for something or someone? What provoked this feeling in you? Did you do anything as a result?

2. What does "universe of responsibility" mean? What individuals and groups do you include in your universe of responsibility? Why? How does your universe of responsibility influence the choices you make about how to treat others?

3. Philosopher John Ruskin said, "What we think or what we know or what we believe is, in the end, of little consequence. The only consequence is what we do." How might Nicholas Kristof respond to Ruskin's argument? What do you think of this statement?

4. Historian Leni Yahil divides knowledge into three parts: receipt of information, acknowledgment of information, and action based on that information.[13] How does Yahil's division of knowledge apply to the way people have responded to more recent humanitarian crises, such as the genocide in Darfur? What do they think can be done, if anything, to move people from receiving information to acting on that information? How would Nicholas Kristof and Paul Slovic answer this question?

5. What is psychic numbing? Under what conditions is psychic numbing helpful? Under what conditions is psychic numbing harmful? Identify a time when you may have experienced psychic numbing—when you may have felt numb to disturbing information and images. Why do you think you felt numb to this information? What could have been done, if anything, to get you to pay thoughtful attention to this information?

6. According to researcher Paul Slovic, studies show that people are more likely to help one person than many people. How do your observations and experiences support and/or refute Slovic's findings? According to Paul Slovic and Nicholas Kristof, what galvanizes people to take action on behalf of others? Think about a time when you were motivated to help someone else. What inspired these actions? Based on your own experiences and on research about human behavior, what are five possible ways to galvanize the public to take action on behalf of others?

7. When suggesting what is needed to prevent genocide and mass murder, Nicholas Kristof writes, "[M]aybe what we need isn't better laws but more troubled consciences." On the other hand, Paul Slovic argues that "we cannot depend only upon our moral feelings to motivate us to take proper actions against genocide." He recommends stronger international laws to prevent and stop large-scale acts of violence. What is the relationship between compassion and law? How can empathy ("moral feelings") and laws be used together to prevent genocide?

8. What has motivated you to feel empathy or compassion for others? In her book *High Tide in Tucson* (1996), Barbara Kingsolver highlights how art, especially storytelling, can be used to get people to care about others. She writes:

> The power of fiction is to create empathy. It lifts you away from your chair and stuffs you gently down inside someone else's point of view. . . . A newspaper could tell you that one hundred people, say, in an airplane, or in Israel, or in Iraq, have died today. And you can think to yourself, "How very sad," then turn the page and see how the Wildcats fared. But a novel could take just one of those hundred lives and show you exactly how it felt to be that person rising from bed in the morning, watching the desert light on the tile of her doorway and on the curve of her daughter's cheek. You could taste that person's breakfast, and love her family, and sort through her worries as your own, and know that a death in that household will be the end of the only life that someone will ever have. As important as yours. As important as mine. . . . Art is the antidote that can call us back from the edge of numbness, restoring the ability to feel for another.[14]

To what extent do you agree with Kingsolver's statement? When has art—a movie, play, story, song, painting, etc.—ever motivated you to feel compassion for someone else? Why do you think this piece had this effect on you?

---

1. Gregory H. Stanton, "About Genocide," International Association of Genocide Scholars, Genocide Watch, 2002, http://www.genocidescholars.org/about.

2. Quoted in Macief Kozlowski, "The Mission that Failed: A Polish Courier Who Tried to Help the Jews," in *My Brother's Keeper? Recent Polish Debates on the Holocaust*, ed. Antony Polonsky (Routledge, 1990), 83.

3. Nicholas Kristof, "Save the Darfur Puppy," *New York Times*, May 10, 2007.

4. Robert J. Lifton, *The Nazi Doctors: Medical Killing and the Psychology of Genocide* (Basic Books, 1986), 442, http://www.holocaust-history.org/lifton/LiftonT442.shtml.

5. *Conversations with History*, Robert Jay Lifton Interview, Institute of International Studies, UC Berkeley, November 2, 1999, http://globetrotter.berkeley.edu/people/Lifton/lifton-con3.html.

6. Barbara Kingsolver, *High Tide in Tucson: Essays from Now or Never* (New York, Harper Perennial, 1996), 232.

7. Leni Yahil, Ina Friedman, and Haya Galai, *The Holocaust: The Fate of European Jewry, 1932–1944* (Oxford University Press, 1991), 545.

8. Kreisler, Harry, "*Evil, the Self, and Survival: Conversation with Robert Jay Lifton, M.D.*," Institute of International Studies, UC Berkeley, Nov. 2, 1999. http://globetrotter.berkeley.edu/people/Lifton/lifton-con3.html.

9. *Reporter*, (00:36:25).

10. Nicholas Kristof, "Save the Darfur Puppy."

11. Paul Slovic, "If I Look at the Mass I Will Never Act: Psychic Numbing and Genocide," *Judgment and Decision Making*, no. 2 (April 2007), http://journal.sjdm.org/7303a/jdm7303a.htm.

12. Chart in Slovic (2007), reprinted from Small et al. (2007), with permission from Elsevier.

13. Leni Yahil, Ina Friedman, and Haya Galai, *The Holocaust*, 544.

14. Kingsolver, *High Tide in Tucson*, 231–232.

INVESTIGATION TWO
Should reporters advocate? Exploring the role of journalists

The readings in this investigation have been selected to deepen our understanding of ideas presented in chapters 10 through 13 (46:18–1:01:40) of the documentary *Reporter* (approximately 15 minutes). In this clip, we are introduced to Yohanita, a dying Congolese woman who becomes the focus for Nicholas Kristof's editorial "A Student, a Teacher and a Glimpse of War." Where Kristof sees a subject for his column about the victims of war in Congo, Leana Wen, a medical student, sees a patient in need of care.

Overview

In "A Student, a Teacher and a Glimpse of War," Nicholas Kristof asks the reader, "How can you walk away from a human being who will surely die if you do so?" Why does he include this language in his editorial? Speaking to journalism students, Kristof mentioned that the goal of his column is to "make people spill their coffee when they read it, then go volunteer or donate" to help solve the problems he writes about.[1] Is this the role of a journalist? Should a reporter be in the business of advocacy—of attempting to influence public policy and individual behavior?

In the interview excerpted below, Brooke Gladstone, host of the show *On the Media*, refers to Kristof as an "advocacy journalist." According to journalism professor Robert Jensen,

> The term "advocacy journalism" typically is used to describe the use of techniques to promote a specific political or social cause. The term is potentially meaningful only in opposition to a category of journalism that does not engage in advocacy, so-called "objective journalism."[2]

But just what is meant by "objective journalism"? Brent Cunningham, editor of the *Columbia Journalism Review*, presents the challenges of answering this question:

> Ask ten journalists what objectivity means and you'll get ten different answers. Some, like the *Washington Post*'s editor, Leonard Downie, define it so strictly that they refuse to vote lest they be forced to take sides. My favorite definition was from Michael Bugeja, who teaches journalism at Iowa State: "Objectivity is seeing the world as it is, not how you wish it were."[3]

Communications professor Richard Taflinger understands the desire for "neutral" or "objective" reporting. He explains, "Such objectivity can allow people to arrive at decisions about the world and events occurring in it without the journalist's subjective views influencing the acceptance or rejection of information."[4]

Kristof "flinches" when Gladstone calls him an advocacy journalist. He worries that advocates are perceived as "somebody who goes out and finds evidence to buttress their preexisting convictions." Advocacy journalist Sean Condon counters this concern by stressing the importance of accuracy. "You still have a responsibility to be telling the truth," he says, "and if you sacrifice that to advocate on behalf of something, you might be doing more damage than help."[5] Kristof maintains a similar approach to his writing. "What I want to do is shine my light to illuminate that problem," he explains, "but I don't want to tinker with the evidence. I just want to galvanize people by showing them what is out there."

"Showing them what is out there," however, requires making choices about what to include and what to leave out. This is why Taflinger refers to objectivity in journalism as "an unrealizable dream."[6] Robert Jensen agrees with him. He argues:

> All reporters use a framework of analysis to understand the world and report on it. But reporting containing open references to underlying political assumptions and conclusions seems to engage in advocacy, while the more conventional approach appears neutral. . . . Accounts of the world, including journalistic ones, must begin from some assumptions about the way the world works. None is neutral.[7]

If no reporting can be purely objective or neutral, then at what point does an article move from news reporting to advocacy? Where along this continuum would we place Kristof's work? How do we account for the fact that Kristof is a columnist whose articles appear on the opinion page of the paper? This role may give him more leeway to advocate on behalf of a cause than a traditional news reporter has, a distinction that Rebecca Hamilton, a reporter for the *Washington Post*, points out. In her role as special correspondent for Sudan, she explains, she is not an activist, even though she cares deeply about stopping the violence in Darfur. Before becoming a reporter, Hamilton spent years working in Sudan and the United States on behalf of victims of the genocide in Darfur. This experience gives her a unique perspective on the role of a reporter. She explains:

> As an activist, one of the most valuable tools in my arsenal was quality reporting from those who were perceived as objective. Whoever you are pushing knows you have an agenda and sometimes can discount your claims because of that. Being able to point to objective reporting that backs up your point is very powerful.

Therefore, Hamilton tries to keep her writing as objective as possible. She refers to an article she wrote about the expulsion of aid workers in Sudan that was used by humanitarian organizations and advocacy groups because it "said things that these organizations were unable to say themselves." By finding hard-to-get perspectives and delivering this information to a broad audience, Hamilton feels she can use her position to help the people in Darfur.

> "On so many of the issues that I care deeply about, the reason that they're not being addressed is simply because they're not on the agenda. And shining a spotlight and making people uncomfortable about what they see in that spotlight, I think, truly is the first step toward getting more resources and more attention and more energy dedicated to solving them."[8]
> – Nicholas Kristof

Reading Kristof's columns and learning about his method of storytelling gives us the opportunity to get to know one model for how journalists can use their role to confront violence and injustice around the world. But this is not the only model. If you were a reporter, how would you choose to use your public voice? What would you want to write about? For what purpose?

Reading 3: "A Student, a Teacher and a Glimpse of War"[9]

The following editorial was written by columnist Nicholas Kristof and published in the *New York Times* opinion section on June 21, 2007.

NICHOLAS D. KRISTOF

A Student, a Teacher and a Glimpse of War

MALEHE, Congo

I'm taking a student, Leana Wen, and a teacher, Will Okun, along with me on this trip to Africa. Here in this thatch-roofed village in the hills of eastern Congo, we had a glimpse of war, and Leana suddenly found herself called to perform.

Villagers took what looked like a bundle of rags out of one thatch-roof hut and laid it on the ground. Only it wasn't a bunch of rags; it was a woman dying of starvation.

The woman, Yohanita Nyiahabimama, 41, weighed perhaps 60 pounds. She was conscious and stared at us with bright eyes, whispering answers to a few questions. When she was moved, she screamed in pain, for her buttocks were covered with ulcerating bedsores.

Leana, who had just graduated from medical school at Washington University, quickly examined Yohanita.

"If we don't get her to a hospital very soon, she will die," Leana said bluntly. "We have to get her to a hospital."

There was nothing special about Yohanita except that she was in front of us. In villages throughout the region, people just like her are dying by the thousands — of a deadly mixture of war and poverty.

Instead of spending a few hundred dollars trying to save Yohanita, who might die anyway, we could spend that money buying vaccines or mosquito nets to save a far larger number of children in other villages.

And yet — how can you walk away from a human being who will surely die if you do so?

So we spoke to Simona Pari of the Norwegian Refugee Council, which has built a school in the village and helped people here survive as conflict has raged around them. Simona immediately agreed to use her vehicle to transport Yohanita to a hospital.

Leana saves a patient in Africa.

The village found a teenage girl who could go with Yohanita and help look after her, and the family agreed that it would be best to have her taken not to the local public hospital but to the fine hospital in Goma run by Heal Africa, an outstanding aid group with strong American connections (www.healafrica.org).

Reading continues on next page.

Now, nearly four days later, Yohanita is on the road to recovery, lying on a clean bed in the Heal Africa Hospital. Leana saved one of her first patients.

What almost killed Yohanita was starvation in a narrow sense, but more broadly she is one more victim of the warfare that has already claimed four million lives in Congo since 1998. Even 21st-century wars like Congo's — the most lethal conflict since World War II — kill the old-fashioned way, by starving people or exposing them to disease.

That's what makes wars in the developing world so deadly, for they kill not only with guns and machetes but also in much greater numbers with diarrhea, malaria, AIDS and malnutrition.

The people here in Malehe were driven out of their village by rampaging soldiers in December. Yohanita's family returned to their home a few months later, but their crops and livestock had been taken. Then Yohanita had a miscarriage and the family spent all its money saving her — which meant that they ran out of food.

"We used to have plenty to eat, but now we have nothing," Yohanita's mother, Anastasie, told us. "We've had nothing to eat but bananas since the beginning of May." (To see video of our visit and read blogs by Leana and Will, go to nytimes.com/twofortheroad.)

I'm under no delusion that our intervention makes a difference to Congo (though it did make quite a difference to Yohanita). The way to help Congo isn't to take individual starving people to the hospital but to work to end the war — yet instead the war is heating up again here, in part because Congo is off the world's radar.

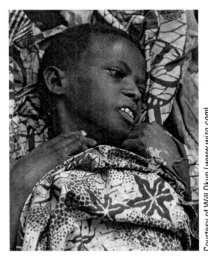

Yohanita, like millions of others in Congo, suffered as a result of armed conflict in the region.

One measure of the international indifference is the shortage of aid groups here: Neighboring Rwanda, which is booming economically, is full of aid workers. But this area of eastern Congo is far needier and yet is home to hardly any aid groups. World Vision is one of the very few American groups active here in the North Kivu area.

Just imagine that four million Americans or Europeans had been killed in a war, and that white families were starving to death as a result of that war. The victims in isolated villages here in Congo, like Yohanita, may be black and poor and anonymous, but that should make this war in Congo no less an international priority. ☐

Reading 4: *On the Media*[10]

The following is an excerpt from Brooke Gladstone's interview with Nicholas Kristof on the public radio program *On the Media* (December 2009).

> **BROOKE GLADSTONE:** So you wrote in *Outside Magazine* recently that you had a revelation when it came to covering Darfur in 2004, but it was coming back that opened your eyes to coverage of Pale Male.
>
> **NICHOLAS KRISTOF:** That's right. At the same time that I was so frustrated by the lack of response to genocide, I found a cause that New Yorkers really could rally around, and that was the eviction of a red-tailed hawk called Pale Male. The building in which he was living had taken down his nest, and New Yorkers were galvanized. And I was just thinking, you know, if only we could get as much indignation and action to prevent genocide as we could about a homeless red-tailed hawk. And that kind of got me thinking about how one can make that connection.
>
> **BROOKE GLADSTONE:** And so you looked at some recent research about what moves us, information that's a big part of marketing.
>
> **NICHOLAS KRISTOF:** Well, I came across social psychologist Paul Slovic, who has done a great deal of work in this area, and the experiments typically involve exposing people to a particular scenario and then seeing if they will contribute. One of the classic experiments involves a seven-year-old girl from the country of Mali who's starving and asking if people will help her out. Everybody wants to help Rokia. But if you ask people to help 21 million hungry people in Africa, nobody particularly wants to help them. Maybe what I found even more depressing is that the moment you even provide more background information [on] Rokia, if you say that she is hungry because of a famine in her country, then interest in helping her tends to drop. You know, we all know that at some point people tend to get numbed and tune out, but one of the things that I found fascinating was the number at which we tend to tune out. It's not a million, it's not a thousand, it's not even a hundred—it's two.
>
> **BROOKE GLADSTONE:** Two! It was just amazing to me to read that. You've got starving little Rokia. You add her starving brother, and people are less likely to support.
>
> **NICHOLAS KRISTOF:** That's right. Even though people are very generous in supporting either Rokia or the boy, Moussa, the moment you put them together, they're less willing to help just two seven-year-old kids. And, you know, so the moment we start talking about hundreds of thousands, people's eyes just glaze over. . . .
>
> **BROOKE GLADSTONE:** How do you finesse a story that might not end happily? Because,

obviously, you're an advocacy journalist; you report not just to report but to spur action. . . . So you've been writing that these sorts of rules—an emphasis on individuals rather than groups, not worrying so much about context, putting the spotlight on positive stories—that these are being heeded by companies trying to sell soap more than they are by philanthropic organizations.

NICHOLAS KRISTOF: You know, at the end of the day I think humanitarians really feel very awkward and embarrassed about marketing, but it really doesn't matter whether a shampoo gets better marketing. It does matter when a famine or a huge crisis is—well, I hate to use the [term] "marketed better," but, you know, is publicized in a way that will be more effective.

BROOKE GLADSTONE: Have you seen a product with no social significance be marketed according to these rules?

NICHOLAS KRISTOF: Sure. I mean, any time you see a shampoo, for example, being marketed, it's not based on the fact that, you know, 38 percent of adults have shinier hair when they use this product. It's about, you know, one particular person who—wow, she looks better and she's going to get a better date or whatever it may be. It's these individual stories that feel kind of empowering and heartwarming. I mean, one of the challenges for me, frankly, is that if you follow this research, then you would leave out context. All you would do would be telling individual stories, and that would be one step too far for me. I do want to connect with people and inform them about these larger problems. So my compromise is that I do try to find a story that will resonate with people. But then at that point I try to throw in the larger context, the background information, and make it clear, in the case of the Congo, for example, how many millions of people are affected and hope that doesn't deter the power of that individual story. . . .

BROOKE GLADSTONE: You said that you flinch when you get called an advocacy journalist, but when you sit down to write a column, what is it that you're trying to achieve?

NICHOLAS KRISTOF: Yeah. Well, I'm advocating. But I'm reluctant to be called out on it. My career was as a reporter, and there's an uncomfortable tension there, because one of the reasons that I became a journalist is, frankly, that I wanted to make a difference. And yet, at the same time, there is sometimes a perception that an advocate is somebody who goes out and finds evidence to buttress their preexisting convictions. And that's why I flinch.

BROOKE GLADSTONE: But you can tell the truth and still want to spark a particular action.

NICHOLAS KRISTOF: Yes, absolutely. That is one of the great perks of journalism, that there are a lot of problems in the world and that we carry a spotlight. What I want to do is shine my light to illuminate that problem, but I don't want to tinker with the evidence. I just want to galvanize people by showing them what is out there.

Connections

1. If you had the opportunity to interview Nicholas Kristof, what would you want to ask him?

2. *Handbook for Citizen Journalists* defines advocacy journalism as "a genre of journalism that adopts a viewpoint for the sake of advocating on behalf of a social, political, business, or religious purpose. It is journalism with an intentional and transparent bias."[11] Based on this definition, what is the difference, if anything, between advocacy journalism and propaganda?

3. What does the phrase "objective reporting" mean to you? Communications professor Richard Taflinger argues that that objectivity is "an unrealizable dream." Do you agree with him? Why or why not?

4. Brooke Gladstone refers to Kristof as an "advocacy journalist." Where, if at all, do you see examples of advocacy in the editorial "A Student, a Teacher and a Glimpse of War"? What is Kristof advocating? In her article "Does 'Caring' Require Advocacy in Journalism?," journalist Elecia Chrunik provides some warnings to writers and readers regarding advocacy journalism:

   > There can be negative consequences to advocacy journalism, like any form of journalism, when it is not done responsibly. . . . Becoming involved with a cause blurs the lines of a journalist's duties and responsibilities. The public might have a difficult time accepting and trusting that journalists are both promoters and truth-tellers. And there are many ways that a journalist can abuse his or her power if he or she feels that the ends justify the means.[12]

   What arguments does Chrunik make about advocacy journalism? How might Kristof respond to these arguments?

5. Nicholas Kristof is a columnist; his job is to write opinion pieces that appear on the editorial page. Does this role give him permission to use his articles to advocate for certain policies and behaviors? Why or why not? Why do you think newspapers include opinion pages? What do you think qualifies someone to express an opinion in a newspaper?

6. Kristof said, "We flinch at the idea of marketing a cause. . .[b]ut it could matter tremendously if we could get people to care about, say, malaria."[13] What is the difference, if any, between marketing aimed at consumer goods, such as soda or shampoo, and marketing aimed at getting people to care about social issues? What strategies do advertisers use to make products attractive to buyers? Which of these techniques, if any, are appropriate for activists to use to promote a social or political issue?

7. To find "an individual whose story, in essence, will inspire the most outrage in his readers over breakfast," *Reporter* filmmaker Eric Metzgar says that Kristof often talks to 50 to 100 people a day. Here is how Metzgar describes finding Yohanita, the subject of the editorial "A Student, a Teacher and a Glimpse of War":

When we found her, Nick had sort of found his Rokia. . . . This is the woman who is going to represent the crisis in Congo. Because he had disregarded a few hundred people's terrible stories and he really found the one that, even to the crew and everyone around, crushed us the most, devastated us the most. But also, the way that. . .Nick told it in his column, it really inspired you the most. And it told the story politically of what was happening in the area. That's important, too.

How did the story of Yohanita impact you? What feelings and ideas did it spark for you? What does the story of Yohanita reveal about conditions in Congo? About three weeks after the *New York Times* published "A Student, a Teacher and a Glimpse of War," Yohanita died from an infection she had when she was brought to the hospital. How does your response to this column change, if at all, knowing that Yohanita did not survive?

8. "What is the greater goal of journalism?" Filmmaker Eric Metzgar asked this question when traveling in Congo with Kristof to produce the *Reporter* documentary. In an interview about his experience making this film, Metzgar describes the tension between writing about suffering and intervening to end the suffering:

> Journalism exists because everyone can't be there to witness it. Right? So we've designated these few people about whom we say, "They're not going to help out. They're not going to intervene. They're simply going to watch and tell people who don't know about it." And that's a strange reality when you're there. To wake up and read the newspaper or read it online is one thing. But when you're there, the idea that you should simply document the story is very strange.[14]

Metzgar says that Kristof probably would not have intervened to get Yohanita to the hospital if Leana Wen, the medical student, had not been on the trip with him. What do you think about Kristof's decision to intervene in this instance? Is this part of his job as a reporter? Is it part of his responsibility as a human being? How do you think journalists should respond to human suffering before their eyes when they are reporting?

---

1. Stig Arlid Pettersen, "Nic Kristof: Balancing the Fine Line Between Journalism and Advocacy," *The Morningside Post at Columbia University*, April 14, 2010,
http://themorningsidepost.com/2010/04/nic-kristof-balancing-the-fine-line-between-journalism-and-advocacy.

2. Robert Jensen, "Advocacy Journalism," in *The International Encyclopedia of Communication*, ed. Wolfgang Donsbach, (Hoboken, NJ, Blackwell Publishing, 2008).

3. Brent Cunningham, "Re-thinking Objectivity," *Colombia Journalism Review* (April 16, 2006), http://www.rdillman.com/Dillman/Courses/COMCommon/articles/news/Re-thinking%20Objectivity.pdf.

4. Richard F. Taflinger, "The Myth of Objectivity in Journalism: A Commentary," May 29, 1996, http://www.wsu.edu/~taflinge/mythobj.html.

5. Elecia Chrunik, "Does 'Caring' Require Advocacy in Journalism?," Center for Journalism Ethics, June 16, 2008, http://www.journalismethics.ca/feature_articles/does_caring_require_advocay.html.

6. Richard F. Taflinger, "The Myth of Objectivity in Journalism: A Commentary."

7. Robert Jensen, "Beyond Advocacy v. Objective Journalism: Who Is Really Objective?," *MediaBite* (Ireland), July 3, 2007, http://uts.cc.utexas.edu/~rjensen/freelance/beyondadvocacy.htm.

8. "Nicholas Kristof on Journalism & Compassion," *Krista Tippet on Being*, September 23, 2010, http://being.publicradio.org/programs/2010/journalism-and-compassion/transcript.shtml.

9. Nicholas Kristof, "A Student, a Teacher and a Glimpse of War," *New York Times*, June 21, 2007.

10. "Follow for Now," Interview with Nick Kristof, *On the Media*, WNYC, December 11, 2009, http://www.onthemedia.org/transcripts/2009/12/11/03.

11. Jack Driscoll, "*Handbook for Citizen Journalists: Catching the Journalistic Attitude*," May 11, 2010, (e-book available from http://www.citizenjournalistnow.com).

12. Elecia Chrunik, "Does 'Caring' Require Advocacy in Journalism?"

13. Stig Arlid Pettersen, "Nic Kristof: Balancing the Fine Between Journalism and Accuracy."

14. "Transcript: Caring About Congo," *NOW on PBS*, February 12, 2010, http://www.pbs.org/now/shows/607/transcript.html.

INVESTIGATION THREE
What do we learn from the news? How reporters' choices shape our understanding of the world

The readings in this investigation have been selected to deepen our understanding of the ideas presented in chapters 13 through 17 (1:01:40–1:19:38) of the documentary *Reporter* (approximately 20 minutes). In this clip, Nicholas Kristof, Will Okun, and Leana Wen travel to the headquarters of General Laurent Nkunda, leader of a rebel militia fighting against the Congolese government and known for perpetrating war crimes. Kristof interviews Nkunda about his role in the civil war and is then granted the opportunity to interview child soldiers captured by Nkunda's army.

Overview

According to journalist Elecia Chrunik, "The outcome of a [news] story is based on a myriad of decisions, and a journalist, good intentions or not, has to face thousands of decisions with every story."[1] Which details should be included? Which should be left out? What should be emphasized? What criteria should reporters use when making these decisions?

Nicholas Kristof has been criticized for focusing on the most negative stories about Africa and casting "a very downbeat light on an entire region."[2] Richard Dowden, author of the book *Africa: Altered States, Ordinary Miracles*, argues, "The media's problem is that, by covering only disasters and wars, it gives us only that image of the continent."[3] Kristof responds to this argument using the media's coverage of Congo as an example:

> My own take is that we in the news media and in the aid world can and should do a much better job providing context and acknowledging successes. Yet the problem surely isn't that the news media have overdone coverage of the disasters. Congo is the most lethal conflict since World War II, costing about five million lives since 1998, and it has dragged on partly because journalists haven't done a better job propelling it onto the international agenda. You'll never persuade me that we've overcovered the slaughter in Congo—our sin is that we didn't scream enough, not that we screamed too much.[4]

While the limited coverage of Congo does tend to focus on "disasters and wars," these accounts do not present events in exactly the same way. We have selected four published accounts about the situation in eastern Congo written between June and November 2007. The first reading, "Dinner with a Warlord," is an editorial written by Kristof. The next two readings are blog entries written by the college student, Leana Wen, and teacher, Will Okun, who accompanied Kristof on this trip to Congo. The last article, "3-Way Battles Again Jolt Eastern Congo," comes from the world news section of a prominent newspaper and would be classified as news reporting. After reviewing each text, consider these questions: What information does it provide? What feelings, ideas, and questions does it elicit? What impression of Congo does it imprint in your mind? What do you think the author's purpose was when creating this piece?

While traveling with Kristof in Congo, teacher Will Okun did not only blog; he also photographed his experience. As he wrote in his winning application essay for the "Win a Trip with Nick" contest,

> While America is only presented with images representative of Africa's poverty and misery, I will seek stories and photographs that will offer our young people a more comprehensive depiction of African people and culture. . . . I hope to produce photographs and stories that will emote pleasure and pride from the Africans themselves.[5]

In a video blog recorded at the end of his trip, Okun reports that he achieved his goal of capturing images that offer a different impression of Congo than that of the war-torn nation depicted by most news media. He hopes his images* "could be taken anywhere," explaining,

> The poverty in the countries that we visited is overwhelming. People can tell you about the poverty, but really until you see it firsthand it's incomprehensible, and it is truly unfair for human beings to be forced to live in these types of conditions. But within the poverty, I was struck by the spirit of the people. So, despite all that poverty, I hope to show the students that I work with that we share the same Earth with these people and that what the students in Chicago have in common with the young people in Africa, what they share in common, is greater and more important than the differences between them.[6]

Four of the images Okun captured are included in Reading 9. When you look at them, what do you see? What do they tell you about Congo? What is universal about them? What feelings or memories do they call up for you?

> "Some see media literacy as a citizenship survival skill, necessary to be a thoughtful consumer and effective citizen in a superhighway-driven media age."[7]
> – Dr. Renee Hobbs, founder of the Media Education Lab and professor at Temple University School of Communications

Each of the texts included in this investigation was created by someone for a specific reason—to inform, to persuade, to galvanize, etc. Being able to identify the author's purpose is an important component of media literacy. So is being able to access and synthesize information from a variety of sources. When we practice analyzing and synthesizing media, we hone a valuable civic skill. Renee Hobbs, author of the article "Building Citizenship Skills through Media Literacy Education," agrees. She writes, "Some see media literacy as a citizenship survival skill, necessary to be a thoughtful consumer and an effective citizen in a superhighway-driven media age."[8]

Why has the rise of the Internet made media literacy a "citizenship survival skill"? For one, we now have access to far more information from a range of authors. The Internet now hosts over 10 million blogs, in addition to social networking sites, citizen journalism websites, and video-sharing sites.[9] Indeed, as the website PBS MediaShift** says about the growing role of "citizen journalists,"

---

* You can view Will Okun's photographs at *www.wjzo.com*. For the pictures he took on his trip with Kristof, click on the link "c.africa."
** See *www.pbs.org/mediashift*.

Because of the wide dispersion of so many excellent tools for capturing live events—from tiny digital cameras to videophones—the average citizen can now make news and distribute it globally, an act that was once the province of established journalists and media companies.[10]

The blogs written by Leana Wen and Will Okun might be considered examples of citizen journalism.

This trend of citizen journalism is not limited to adults. Young people are also publishing their ideas about the world around them. Researchers on youth and digital media at the Good Play Project have found that "[f]ar from being passive consumers (or, as some fear, victims) of new media, young people are actively contributing to and defining the new media landscape through sites such as Facebook, MySpace, Flickr, YouTube, [and] Second Life as well as blogs and multi-player games."[11] While youth are clearly developing the practical know-how to navigate the media superhighway, these researchers ask if young people are developing an ethical sense regarding how they create and consume media. What does it mean to use media in a responsible way? How do we know what information to trust? What criteria should we use? Where do we learn how to make moral choices about the words and images we publish? These are some questions to consider as you explore the following texts and as you use media in your daily life.

Reading 5: "Dinner with a Warlord"[12]

The following editorial was written by columnist Nicholas Kristof and published in the *New York Times* opinion section on June 18, 2007.

NICHOLAS D. KRISTOF

Dinner With A Warlord

A HILLTOP IN EASTERN CONGO
One hint that this would be an unusual interview came when the warlord walked in wearing a button reading "Rebels For Christ."

Then when I reached to sip the café au lait that the guerrilla leaders offered me in their jungle redoubt, they looked reproachful and quickly bowed their heads and said grace.

I'm taking a student and a teacher along on a reporting trip to Africa, and we wanted to look at how civil wars tear countries apart and block the continent's economic development. So we rented a jeep and drove past the last checkpoints outside the city of Goma, and then jounced along a tortuous dirt road into the hills.

We traveled through gorgeous green hills and forests, thatch-roof villages and mist-shrouded canyons. Government is only a rumor here, for the capital is 1,200 miles away and has no control in the east and offers no services. There is no postal service, no national health or education system, no authority to rein in the ultimate boss in the third world: a man with a gun.

Along the way to see the warlord,

A war that's not playing at your local theater.

we stopped at an elementary school. It is financed by the parents, who pay $9 per year per child to the eight teachers who instruct 520 students. Many parents cannot afford that sum, so they keep their children at home.

The school building hadn't been kept up since the Belgians ruled Congo in the years before 1960. The Belgians were brutal colonial masters in Congo, but after enduring subsequent rounds of kleptocratic incompetence and civil war, some Congolese feel nostalgic for the lesser tyranny of colonialism.

Finally we were stopped by a band of soldiers who searched us carefully and then led us past more guards with AK-47s and grenade launchers to the sanctum of Laurent Nkunda, the chieftain of a swath of war-torn eastern Congo.

Mr. Nkunda, 40, is a smart and charismatic man with a university education who treated us to several hours of lively conversation in his fluent English, followed by a tasty chicken dinner. He described himself as a devout Pentecostal and said that most of his troops had converted as well; he showed us a church where he said they pray daily, and he showed photos of baptisms of the soldiers.

Then again, the government has issued an international arrest warrant against him for war crimes, and human rights monitors like Refugees International say that his troops have killed and raped civilians and pillaged their villages. He denies the charges.

"I'm not a warlord... I'm a liberator of the people," he said.

That's the problem: So are they all.

More than four million people have died in Congo's wars since 1998, making it the most lethal conflict since World War II.

Probably no slaughter has gotten fewer column inches — or fewer television minutes — per million deaths. So even after all that suffering, Congo still hasn't risen to a prominent place on the international agenda.

That's why I came here with Leana Wen and Will Okun, the student and teacher from my win-a-trip contest. (Video and photos of the trip and blogs by Will and Leana are at nytimes.com/twofortheroad.)

The U.N. did hold elections last year, and much of Congo is indeed more stable today. But here in this region of eastern Congo, a wretched situation is getting even worse.

Since January about 150,000 people have been driven from their homes by renewed violence, and there are widespread fears that a larger war is looming.

"We see war coming," Mr. Nkunda said, and he pulled out his laptop to show a map indicating that various government-backed forces are being dispatched to attack him. He added: "The only reply to war and ammunition is war and ammunition."

I told him — a bit nervously — that such tribalism and fighting has torn apart a country that should be one of Africa's richest. But Mr. Nkunda, who quotes Gandhi, emphasized that what counts here is simply force. "You go by strength," he said.

There are no easy solutions here, although some steps are essential: supporting professional training and reform of the Congolese security forces, pressuring neighboring Rwanda to support central authority over the full country, bolstering the peace process, and interdicting mineral exports that finance rebel armies. But the most important step is simply for the international community to acknowledge that a war that costs four million lives must be an international priority, even if the victims aren't staring at us from television screens. ☐

Paul Krugman is on vacation.

General Laurent Nkunda, rebel leader in eastern Congo, considers himself a "liberator of the people." He was arrested in 2009. The Congolese government plans to try him for war crimes committed in the country.

Reading 6: "Killing in the Name of God"[13]

The following post was written by medical student Leana Wen and published on June 21, 2007, on the *New York Times* blog *Two for the Road: In Africa with Nick Kristof* (twofortheroad.blogs.nytimes.com).

> Killing in the Name of God
> Posted by: L. Wen   Date: 06/21/2007
>
> The most bizarre experience on this trip so far has been the visit to General Laurent Nkunda. It's hardly an everyday occurrence to go to the military camp of an actual "warlord" who is accused of raping and massacring thousands. (He prefers to be referred to as "liberator of the people" and denies all allegations against him.) . . .
>
> One of the most striking parts of the interview is the religious fervor with which General Nkunda led his troops. Apparently, he is very influenced by the evangelist movement, and as a pastor in the Pentecostal church, he helps to convert and baptize his troops. He proudly sported a pin, "Rebels for Christ." Before each drink and meal, he and his faithful prayed. "We fight in the name of the Lord," he told us. "That is what I tell all my troops. When they fight, they have God on their side."
>
> As a lapsed Christian, I have to admit that I don't know much about Christianity. But something about Nkunda's comments made me feel ill to my stomach. Was he really using God as a license to kill? Was it really his conviction that God was with him in battle, or was he using "the God card" as a way to manipulate and control his troops? It would not be the first time that the name of God has been used to consolidate power, and certainly not the first time religion has given hope and purpose to unemployed young men without good futures. . . .
>
> I lie awake at night thinking about our experiences in Congo. Meeting this charismatic general who sounds like a preacher is superimposed with seeing the villages destroyed and hearing the stories of those whose lives were cut short because of conflict. To be fair, other "warlords" and rebel groups are also implicated in the conflict. And I may not know much about Christianity, or God. But the basic values of humanity are such that killing and maiming innocent people—in anyone's name—is just wrong. That General Nkunda is able to use religion as a rallying cry to the point of committing such atrocities is testament to the depth of the problems and the erosion of human values in Congo.

Reading 7: "Fear"[14]

The following post was written by high-school teacher Will Okun and published on June 20, 2007, on the *New York Times* blog *Two for the Road: In Africa with Nick Kristof* (twofortheroad.blogs.nytimes.com).

> Fear
> Posted by: W. Okun   Date: 06/20/2007
>
> I can hear the music pulsating in the thick Congo night, inviting me. "Come over, dance, drink, have a good time, enjoy life." But I am scared to leave the hotel at night.
>
> The breaking news is just over those mountains, the stories that will bring attention to the horrific conflicts of Congo. But I am too scared to go. There is fighting in the hills, and everyone says the soldiers on both sides are immoral, unpredictable, and without remorse.
>
> It is terrible to feel such fear, it shakes you to the core. It controls your days and your nights, your security, your freedoms, and even seeps into your dreams. I do not have to live in such fear; in one week I can go home. But such is life in parts of the Democratic Republic of Congo, where various conflicts have killed four million people and displaced one-and-a-half million more since 1998.
>
> Imagine living in a rural community where your daughter could be raped, or even sodomized, by soldiers every time she leaves home. Recently, Nick Kristof asked a village leader to speak with a woman who had been raped, and the line continued to grow and grow at a sickening rate.
>
> Imagine living in a rural community where you do not grow crops to feed your family, because the soldiers will simply eat all the fruits of your labor anyway. Imagine hiding the fact that you have a job, because the soldiers will ransack your house first. Imagine leaving your village and home with your family in the dark of night for places unknown, because the soldiers' violence devours everything in its path.
>
> The gripping control of fear is not exclusive to Congo. I know families in Chicago who do not let their kids outside to play. I have seen children scatter when it was only a car backfiring. I have taught high-school gang members who know any day could also be their last day.

People do not appreciate security until they experience fear. Fear is so encompassing that it can become a person's driving force. It is ludicrous to expect a person, community, or even a nation to prosper and progress when they are in the throes of instability, insecurity, and fear.

Basic human rights like education, health, liberty, etc., cannot be developed and obtained until security is established, whether it be in Congo or in Chicago.

And yet most of us, including myself, are only truly concerned about the security of our loved ones. We do not care about the other side of town, [let alone] the other side of the world. How can I care about wars in Africa when I do not even care enough to combat gang warfare, bad schools, inadequate health care, unsafe water, etc., on the South Side of Chicago? How do I change this mindset, for myself and for others?

Reading 8: "3-Way Battles Again Jolt Eastern Congo"[15]

The following news article was written by reporter Jeffrey Gettleman and published on page A3 of the international section of the *New York Times* on October 25, 2007.

NAIROBI, Kenya—Eastern Congo continues to be wracked by violence, UN officials said yesterday, and battles between rival militias are driving thousands of beleaguered villagers from their homes and complicating the government's efforts to strike a truce.

Sylvie van den Wildenberg, a UN spokeswoman in eastern Democratic Republic of Congo, said a three-sided fight broke out this weekend among the Congolese government and two militias, one allied with government troops and the other fiercely independent. The government is now trying to disarm both militias, but it is not clear if either will submit.

The warfare has turned eastern Congo into a kill zone, and in the past few days tens of thousands of residents have fled. The number of displaced people in just one province, North Kivu, has swelled to more than 750,000.

"It's a catastrophe," van den Wildenberg said. ". . . All these people are running, and no one seems to know where to go."

After Hutu death squads exterminated hundreds of thousands of Tutsis in Rwanda in 1994, many culprits fled into the thickly forested hills of eastern Congo, next door. The Hutu militias have regrouped, and United Nations officials blame them for terrorizing civilians, especially women.

In the past few weeks fighting has raged between the Congolese Army and the forces of Laurent Nkunda, a dissident Tutsi general who has accused the Congolese Army of helping the Hutu militias, a charge the army denies. Nkunda says his men—and boys, because many are child soldiers—are simply protecting the Tutsis in Congo from being massacred.

Joseph Kabila, Congo's president, tried to negotiate with Nkunda. Then, a few weeks ago, Kabila gave him an ultimatum, threatening to wipe out his troops unless they turned in their guns or joined the national army. UN officials said more than 1,200 fighters defected to the government.

But then the Mai-Mai entered the equation. The Mai-Mai are a huge force of loosely organized Congolese militiamen, who have jumped into the fight on the side of the government, saying that Nkunda is a warlord.

On Saturday, as Nkunda's forces battled government troops near the Rwandan border, the Mai-Mai attacked Nkunda from a different direction. Heavy artillery boomed and sent tens of thousands of villagers scattering in the rain. Kabila ordered the Mai-Mai to stand down, but they refused.

Reading 9: Images of Congo

The following four photographs were taken by Will Okun during his trip to Congo in June 2007 and are published on his website, *www.wjzo.com*.

Connections

1. What is the benefit of reviewing multiple sources, written from different perspectives, about the same topic? What are the consequences when we limit ourselves to only one version of events? Given the tremendous amount of information available on the Internet, how do you know when you have accessed enough information to form a thoughtful opinion about a subject?

2. Nicholas Kristof's column is an editorial; Leana Wen and Will Okun wrote blogs; the other stories appeared in the front sections of the newspaper. What information do you assume about media based on its genre (type) and where you find it? Is it important that "news" stories are distinguished from opinion pieces? Why or why not?

3. According to the Center for Journalism Ethics, "The internet has created a new sphere where everyone can be a journalist; all you need is a computer and an opinion—no training necessary."[16] Do you think that only a trained journalist should be reporting the news? Why or why not? When reading a news story, what do you want to know about who wrote it? Why is this information important?

4. What criteria do you use when deciding if you can trust what you are reading, watching, or hearing? If you were writing a news story, blog, or editorial, what could you do to improve your trustworthiness as a writer?

5. When you think of Africa, what images and topics come to mind? Do you think of Africa as one vast continent or as a collection of distinct nations? Do you think of Nobel Prize winners, successful businesses, and thriving agriculture? Why might this be the case? See Africa Differently (*www.seeafricadifferently.com*) is a website dedicated to celebrating the good news coming out of Africa. What is the role of such a website?

6. Richard Dowden argues that journalists like Kristof paint a negative portrait of Africa because they cover only the problems facing the continent. *Reporter* filmmaker Eric Metzgar responds to this argument as follows:

    > My response is that—the way that Nick works is. . .a bit like a surgeon. You know, you don't wanna go in and have your surgeon tell you, "Well, I've looked you over and your elbow is workin' just fine and your vision's great. And come back later." You know, you'd say, "Well, I came here to know what the problems are and what we can do to fix 'em." And so Nick goes in there simply to say, "Look, there's excess suffering happening here. And people are not shining a light on it. Americans are not aware of what's happening, and if they were then maybe they can do something.[17]

    What do you think of Metzgar's argument? What could be the consequences if reporters focus exclusively (or mostly) on the problems facing a community? What could be the consequences if reporters focus exclusively (or mostly) on solutions? What do you suggest as a reasonable compromise for those who want reporters to cover both problems and solutions? How should communities

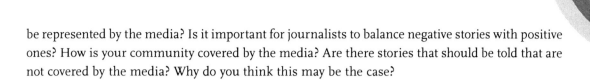

be represented by the media? Is it important for journalists to balance negative stories with positive ones? How is your community covered by the media? Are there stories that should be told that are not covered by the media? Why do you think this may be the case?

7. In an interview with *Teen Ink* magazine, Kristof shares one of his concerns as a reporter. He worries that "focusing on the massacres, and the mass rape, and all the other bad things, I leave people with a misperception of the continent [Africa] as a whole that discourages tourism, that discourages studying abroad, that discourages investment."[18] Do you think this is a valid concern? What could Kristof do so that readers are less likely to hold misperceptions of Africa?

8. In the editorial "Dinner with a Warlord," Kristof complains about the lack of media coverage of Congo:

> More than four million people have died in Congo's wars since 1998, making it the most lethal conflict since World War II. Probably no slaughter has gotten fewer column inches—or fewer television minutes—per million deaths. So even after all that suffering, Congo still hasn't risen to a prominent place on the international agenda.

What gets the most attention in the media, in the newspaper, on television, and on the Internet and social networking sites? What should get the most attention? Why?

9. According to a 2008 survey by the Pew Research Center, most Americans "follow international news only when important developments occur."[19] What can be done to bring attention to ongoing humanitarian crises, like poverty, lack of clean drinking water, the mistreatment of women and girls, etc.?

---

1. Elecia Chrunik, "Does 'Caring' Require Advocacy in Journalism?," Center for Journalism Ethics, June 16, 2008, *http://www.journalismethics.ca/feature_articles/does_caring_require_advocay.html*.

2. "Transcript: Caring About Congo," *NOW on PBS*, February 12, 2010, *http://www.pbs.org/now/shows/607/transcript.html*.

3. Nicholas Kristof, "Bright Continent," *New York Times*, May 1, 2009, *http://www.nytimes.com/2009/05/03/books/review/Kristof-t.html?_r=2*.

4. Ibid.

5. Will Okun, "Winning Essay: Will Okun," *New York Times*, April 29, 2007, accessed September 19, 2010, *http://www.nytimes.com/2007/04/29/opinion/29wat-okun.html*.

6. Will Okun, "Win a Trip: Will's Reflections," *New York Times* video, July 2, 2007, accessed September 10, 2010, *http://video.nytimes.com/video/2007/07/03/opinion/1194817111919/win-a-trip-wills-reflections.html*.

7. Renee Hobbs, "Building Citizenship Skills through Media Literacy Education," Center for Media Literacy, *http://www.medialit.org/reading_room/article365.html*.

8. Renee Hobbs, "Building Citizenship Skills through Media Literacy Education."

9. Carolynne Burkholder, "Citizen Journalism: Blogging," Center for Journalism Ethics, *http://www.journalismethics.ca/citizen_journalism/blogging.htm*.

10. Mark Glaser, "Your Guide to Citizen Journalism," PBS MediaShift, September 27, 2006, accessed September 19, 2010, *http://www.pbs.org/mediashift/2006/09/your-guide-to-citizen-journalism270.html*.

11. "Research Profile: The GoodPlay Project–Overview," 2007, accessed September 19, 2010, *http://www.goodworkproject.org/research/digital.htm*.

12. Nicholas Kristof, "Dinner with a Warlord," *New York Times*, June 18, 2007.

13. Leana Wen, "Killing in the Name of God," *Two for the Road* (blog), June 21, 2007, *http://twofortheroad.blogs.nytimes.com*.

14. Will Okun, "Fear," *Two for the Road* (blog), June 20, 2007, *http://twofortheroad.blogs.nytimes.com*.

15. Jeffrey Gettleman, "3-Way Battles Again Jolt Eastern Congo," *New York Times*, October 25, 2007, *http://www.nytimes/com/2008/01/06/world/africa/06congo.html*.

16. Carolynne Burkholder, "Citizen Journalism."

17. "Transcript: Caring About Congo."

18. Eliza E. and Alicia H., "Journalist Nicholas Kristof," *Teen Ink*, accessed September 19, 2010, *http://www.teenink.com/nonfiction/celebrity_interviews/article/207195/Journalist-Nicholas-Kristof*.

19. "Key News Audiences Now Blend Online and Traditional Sources," The Pew Research Center for the People and the Press, August 17, 2008, *http://people-press.org/report/?pageid=1356*.

INVESTIGATION FOUR
What can we do to help? Education and action

The reading in this investigation has been selected to deepen our understanding of ideas presented in the documentary *Reporter*. As we follow Nicholas Kristof through eastern Congo, we are confronted with many of the problems—including poverty, lack of medical care, and violence—endured by the women, children, and men living in the region.

Overview

In the spring of 2007, Leana Wen, a medical student, applied to win a trip to central Africa with *New York Times* columnist Nicholas Kristof. In her winning essay, she writes, "I want to fight these injustices and change the world." She believes that traveling with Kristof will give her some tools to do this. Wen's desire to fight injustice comes from personal experience. She explains:

> My upbringing exposed me to injustices firsthand. Raised in a dissident family in China, I came to the US on political asylum after the Tiananmen Square massacre.* We were outsiders in a Communist regime and remained outsiders in predominantly Mormon Utah and then inner-city Los Angeles. Though Shanghai, Logan, and Compton have little else in common, they all bear witness to the differences between the haves and have-nots, and I grew up keenly aware of the impact of political, cultural, and socioeconomic oppression. As a child with life-threatening asthma and debilitating speech impediment, I also confronted the stigma of disability and the challenges of seeking health care with limited resources. Yet the mechanisms to address injustices eluded me.[1]

Wen decided to become a doctor so that she could "help those most in need." Yet during her first few years in the medical profession, she "witnessed more problems than found solutions."[2] Frustrated, she arrived at the following belief: "Global change requires more than pills and individual-level change: it hinges on concerted education and mobilization."[3] While in central Africa with Kristof, Wen elaborated on this idea in the blog entry "What Can We Do to Help?" Her broad suggestions—educate yourself, educate others, and take action—can be applied to help solve any problem, from global poverty to

> "I think that there are a lot of young people who are not put off by the vastness of the challenges, but are making these incremental differences in real places. . ."[4]
> – Nicholas Kristof

---

* In 1989, thousands of demonstrators, many of them students, gathered in the largest public square in the world—Tiananmen Square in Beijing—to protest against the Chinese government in favor of democratic reform. The "Tiananmen Square massacre" refers to the government's crackdown on protesters, which resulted in an unknown number of deaths, with estimates ranging from 100 to 3,000 (http://www.nytimes.com/1989/06/21/world/a-reassessment-of-how-many-died-in-the-military-crackdown-in-beijing.html).

neighborhood hate crimes. After reading this blog post, consider the issues that impact your community, problems that provoke your sense of outrage, or causes that you care about. What can you do to help? In particular, how can you use your voice to intervene in the face of injustice? How can you use your role as a consumer and creator of media to prevent future injustice?

Reading 10: "What Can We Do to Help?"

The following post was written by medical student Leana Wen and published on the *New York Times* blog *Two for the Road: In Africa with Nick Kristof* (twofortheroad.blogs.nytimes.com) on June 27, 2007.

Doctor Leana Wen travels around the world learning about global health issues and educating others.

"What Can We Do to Help?"
Posted by: L. Wen Date: 06/27/2007

One of the most common comments we get goes: "What can I do to help? You guys talk so much about the problems, and now I want to do something." I don't like to bring up problems without proposing solutions. In this second-to-last entry, I propose concrete action steps to channel passion and idealism into activism and action.

Be forewarned that I don't think that giving money is usually the best way to help. I believe that education, awareness, and tangible actions multiply many times over. They are actions that, during your lifetime, will far outweigh infrequent monetary contributions. An aid worker at HEAL Africa summarized my thoughts when she said, "It's too easy to give money and feel like you've helped. Doing something shouldn't be about relieving your guilty conscience." That said, there are many humanitarian organizations doing great things that rely on donor funds, and I do hope that you consider supporting them. I am just proposing other ways to help beyond monetary contributions.

1) Educate yourself
Exposure to and understanding of issues is the most important and most fundamental step of "doing something" to help. Broaden your understanding through reading and traveling. Your voice as an activist will be much stronger if assertions are backed by evidence, and if your passion and conviction is grounded in reality. . . .

2) Educate others
Once you understand the issues and have spent time abroad, use your social and professional networks to educate others and share ideas. You have more networks than you might think. Forward articles to help educate family and friends. Join discussion forums. If you worked abroad or spent time researching an issue, seek opportunities in your community to give talks. . . .

3) Take action
Assist existing humanitarian aid groups. There are many excellent aid organizations worthy of your investment or volunteer time. . . . Lobby your legislators. It's not because of politicians that the US is not doing enough to help Africa or to stop the war in Congo. It's because we have not, as a country, expressed interest in global issues. . . . Ultimately it is us who will propel our government to action.

Finally, remember that problems don't exist just in Africa; injustices exist everywhere. Social activism is not limited just to the places "over there"; there are many opportunities to assist no matter where you are. Insecurity is not limited just to war-torn areas; there are destructive people and destructive values that exist in our own backyard. There is a lot we can do by assisting our own communities. Part of being globally conscious involves striving to help all those around us, to the best of our abilities, every single day.

Connections

1. Make an identity chart for Leana Wen.* What do you know about her? How do you think her identity has shaped her goal "to solve global problems by educating and motivating the public to action"?[5] How has your identity shaped your beliefs about civic participation—about being involved in your community (local, national, or global)?

2. Wen's first suggestion is to "educate yourself." What do you want to know more about, in terms of problems facing communities near or far? Where might you look to find this information?

3. Wen writes about the need for people to be "globally conscious." In other words, people should know something about what is happening around the world. Yet despite the rise in access to news, the proportion of young people who do not read or watch the news—online, in print, or on television—has actually increased.[6] Do you think this is a problem? What can be done to get more young people to access the news? Besides watching or reading the news, how else might young people learn about what is going on in the world?

4. In an interview with *Teen Ink* magazine, Kristof offers advice about how we should "educate ourselves" about what is happening in the world:

   > Maybe the biggest thing I would caution against is something that is very human, which is to seek out sources we agree with. There is a deeply ingrained tendency for liberals and conservatives alike to find sources that just seem incredibly reasonable, and tend to be those that confirm our every prejudice. . . . And I think that tends to be bad for democracy and for one's own intellectual development. So, I would encourage students to bite the bullet and go out and seek out intelligent views that challenge the things they hold dear.[7]

   What are the consequences when we only read or watch points of view that affirm our beliefs? Where would you go to seek out views that are different from your own?

5. Wen's second suggestion is for people to "educate others." How might this be done? The website *www.halftheskymovement.org* (a companion to the book *Half the Sky*, written by Nicholas Kristof and Sheryl WuDunn, about the plight of women around the world) provides some ideas. It lists three "simple actions [that] have the potential to reach thousands. . .even millions of people across the planet":

   1) spread the word via social networking,
   2) tell a friend by sharing an email, and
   3) download images and use them on your blog or web page or add them to your email signature.

---

* Learn more about identity charts (*www.facinghistory.org/resources/strategies/identity-charts*) by reading pages 8–9 of *Facing History and Ourselves: Holocaust and Human Behavior* (*www.facinghistory.org/resources/hhb*).

Have you ever done any of these things? What are other ways you can use the Internet to educate others about a cause that is important to you?

6. Leana's final suggestion is to "take action." She reminds us that "problems don't exist just in Africa; injustices exist everywhere." What injustices exist in your community? What is being done about them? If you were going to take action, what could you do to help?

7. Even after learning about a problem, many people do not take action. Why do you think this is the case? What obstacles get in our way? Under what circumstances might someone become motivated to take action? Have you ever been motivated to take action for something you believed in? If so, what motivated your decision to get involved? If not, why do you think that you have never felt inspired to do something on behalf of a cause you care about?

8. How can teenagers play a role in helping to solve world problems? Are those under voting age too young to make a difference? Kristof believes youth can have an impact in addressing world problems. He explains:

> One thing I think today's teenagers are really good at is starting projects that make a difference abroad, instead of supporting some kind of symbolic protest that feels good but doesn't make a specific difference in people's lives. Last night, for example, I met Brittany Young, a young woman who started a group called "A Spring of Hope." In high school she started this group [that] essentially builds wells for schools in Africa. Although this is not going to solve the world's problem of bad water, or solve education problems in Africa, for a few specific schools, it's going to mean they're going to get water where they didn't have it before. That's a real difference, and I think that there are a lot of young people who are not put off by the vastness of the challenges, but are making these incremental differences in real places.[8]

To what extent do you agree or disagree with Kristof's statement? What opportunities exist for teenagers to make "incremental differences in real places"? What might limit the ability of teenagers to have an impact?

---

1. Leana Wen, "Winning Essay: Leana Wen," *New York Times*, April 29, 2007, accessed September 19, 2010, *http://www.nytimes.com/2007/04/29/opinion/29wat-wen.html*.

2. Ibid.

3. Ibid.

4. Eliza E. and Alicia H., "Journalist Nicholas Kristof," *Teen Ink*, accessed September 19, 2010, *http://www.teenink.com/nonfiction/celebrity_interviews/article/207195/Journalist-Nicholas-Kristof*.

5. Ibid.

6. "Key News Audiences Now Blend Online and Traditional Sources," The Pew Research Center for the People and the Press, August 17, 2008, *http://people-press.org/report/444/news-media*.

7. Eliza E. and Alicia H., "Journalist Nicholas Kristof."

8. Ibid.

WEB RESOURCES FOR *REPORTER*

For information related to Nicholas Kristof and the film *Reporter*:

Making Media, Making Sense, Making a Difference (http://reporter.facinghistory.org)
Facing History has developed a website to help students, educators, and community members explore questions about being an engaged global citizen in our information age. The website houses a digital version of "*Teaching* Reporter," as well as additional *Reporter* resources (e.g. streaming film clips, lesson ideas, and interactive polls). This site also presents information about our Digital Media Innovation Network, including student work created by it's members

Two for the Road (http://twofortheroad.blogs.nytimes.com)
This is the blog that Leana Wen and Will Okun kept while traveling with Nicholas Kristof in central Africa. The blog also includes video reflections and links to editorials Kristof wrote during the trip.

Reporter film website (http://www.reporterfilm.com/main.html)
The official website for *Reporter* provides background information about Congo, photos taken during the filming of the documentary, biographies of Nicholas Kristof and the filmmakers, and action steps that might be taken after viewing this film.

Nicholas D. Kristof's *New York Times* opinion page (http://topics.nytimes.com/top/opinion/editorialsandoped/oped/columnists/nicholasdkristof/index.html)
This page provides links to all of Kristof's columns, along with video footage from some of his trips.

On the Ground (http://kristof.blogs.nytimes.com)
Kristof's blog on the *New York Times* website expands on the ideas from his columns. Readers' comments contribute additional insights and questions. You can post your comments here, as well. Kristof can also be followed on Twitter (http://twitter.com/nickkristof) and Facebook (http://www.facebook.com/kristof).

WJZO Photography (http://www.wjzo.com)
This is where Will Okun posts his photographs. Click on "c.africa" to view the images he took on his trip with Kristof.

Caring About Congo (http://www.pbs.org/now/shows/607/index.html)
In February 2010, the PBS show *NOW* interviewed filmmaker Eric Metzgar about his experience making *Reporter*. You can read the transcript of this fascinating interview, watch it as a video, or listen to it as a podcast.

For information related to the Democratic Republic of Congo and Darfur:

Enough Project (http://www.enoughproject.org)
Enough Project was founded to build a permanent constituency to prevent genocide and crimes against humanity. Its members maintain up-to-date resources on the situations in eastern Congo and Darfur.

Ripples of Genocide: Journey through Eastern Congo (http://www.ushmm.org/museum/exhibit/online/congojournal/)
This online exhibit, created by the United States Holocaust Memorial Museum, provides insights into Congo by examining the diaries of four individuals who traveled there in 2003 (including actress Angelina Jolie). The site also has information about the current situation in Congo.

Genocide Intervention Network (http://www.genocideintervention.net)
This advocacy group was founded to empower individuals by giving them the tools to stop and prevent genocide. The website includes background information about Congo and Darfur, as well as ideas about what individuals can do to help restore peace to these regions.

A Promise Unkept (http://www.nytimes.com/packages/khtml/2004/10/20/opinion/20041020_DARFUR_FEATURE.html)
This online presentation about Darfur, narrated by Nicholas Kristof, includes small video clips with topics such as "Why Should We Care?," "America and Genocide," and "What Can We Do?"

Coalition to Stop the Use of Child Soldiers (http://www.child-soldiers.org/home)
This organization works to prevent the recruitment and use of children as soldiers and to secure their rehabilitation. The website provides an array of resources to help the public better understand this issue, including basic facts and the testimony of child soldiers.

For more information about journalism and reporting:

HSJ.org
Published by the ASNE (American Society of News Editors), HSJ.org is one of the leading websites for information about high-school journalism. It includes investigations for students and teachers. In the teachers' section, you can find hundreds of lesson plans and other resources on topics ranging from writing editorials to conducting interviews to copyediting.

Newseum (http://www.newseum.org)
Newseum, located in Washington, DC, was founded for the purpose of "helping people better understand the news and the important role it plays in their lives." Watching *Reporter* would be an appropriate activity before or after visiting this museum. The museum's website hosts helpful resources for teachers, including lesson plans on topics such as "First Amendment" and "Headlines from History," and news stories from different historical eras.

Project for Excellence in Journalism (http://www.journalism.org)
The Pew Research Center's Project for Excellence is a nonpartisan website dedicated to the study

of the press. The website hosts survey results and reports—many of them focused on new media. This is a great site to explore for deeper knowledge about the changing landscape of journalism.

Center for Journalism Ethics for the Global Citizen (*http://www.journalismethics.ca/index.htm*)
The website of the Center for Journalism Ethics at the University of Wisconsin-Madison focuses on advancing the ethical standards of journalism. The center explores ethical issues related to traditional journalism and new media, including blogging and citizen journalism. It also provides links to different examples of journalism ethics codes.

News Writing with Scholastic Editors (*http://teacher.scholastic.com/writewit/news/index.htm*)
This website provides step-by-step instructions to help students write and publish their own news stories.

The News Manual (*http://www.thenewsmanual.net*)
This professional resource for journalists includes three online manuals: *Volume 1: Basic Techniques*, *Volume 2: Advanced Reporting*, and *Volume 3: Ethics and the Law*. For beginners, you might want to start with "The Shape of a Story," which includes an image and description of the inverted pyramid structure for news writing.

Student Reporting Labs (*http://www.studentreportinglabs.com*)
PBS *Newshour* has created a website aimed to help student journalists create and share their work. The website includes information on how to create a student reporting lab that connects with local PBS stations and news professionals, as well as stories produced by students across the country. The *Student Reporting Labs Curriculum* (*http://www.studentreportinglabs.com/reporting-labs-curriculum*) consists of nine lesson plans focused on digital and news literacy.

Credits

Grateful acknowledgment is made for permission to reprint the following:

Map of Congo. Reproduced with permission from Peace Corps World Wise Schools.

Photography by Will Okun, *www.wjzo.com*. Reproduced with permission.

"Follow for Now," *On the Media*. Reprinted with permission from On the Media-WNYC Radio.

The following articles: © 2007 *The New York Times*. All rights reserved. Used by permission and protected by Copyright Laws of the United States. The printing, copying, redistribution, or retransmission of the Material without express written permission is prohibited.

Nicholas Kristof, "Save the Darfur Puppy," *New York Times*, May 10, 2007.

Nicholas Kristof, "A Student, a Teacher and a Glimpse of War," *New York Times*, June 21, 2007.

Nicholas Kristof, "Dinner With a Warlord," *New York Times*, June 18, 2007.

Will Okun, "Fear," *Two for the Road* (blog), June 20, 2007.

Will Okun, "Winning Essay," *New York Times*, April 29, 2007.

Leana Wen, "Killing in the Name of God," *Two for the Road* (blog), June 21, 2007.

Leana Wen, "What Can We Do to Help?," *Two for the Road* (blog), June 27, 2007.

Leana Wen, "Winning Essay," *New York Times*, April 29, 2007.

CPSIA information can be obtained at www.ICGtesting.com
Printed in the USA
BVOW051537250313

316402BV00003B/7/P